Beyond the Book
Theory, Culture, and the Politics of Cyberspace

Edited by Warren Chernaik, Marilyn Deegan, and Andrew Gibson

BOWLING GREEN STATE UNIVERSITY

DISCARDED

LIBRARY

Office for Humanities Communication Publications
Number 7
Published with The Centre for English Studies,
University of London

BOWLING GREEN STATE
UNIVERSITY LIBRARY

Office for Humanities Communication
Humanities Computing Unit
Oxford University Computing Services
13 Banbury Road
Oxford
OX2 6NN
Tel: 01865-273221

First published by the OHC in March 1996

© Office for Humanities Communication
ISBN 1 897791 09 7

Printed by Tony Hunter at Oxford University Computing Services

The Office for Humanities Communication is a national centre focusing on all aspects of information and communication in the humanities, and is funded by the British Library Research and Development Department. The main aims of the OHC are to carry out research on matters of current concern to scholars (both in their teaching and research), learned societies, libraries, and publishers, especially relating to the effects of new technology on communication; promoting awareness and disseminating information about these concerns by means of organizing conferences, meetings, and working parties of experts, and producing printed and online newsletters. The OHC also establishes and maintains contact with relevant bodies in other countries.

Office for Humanities Communication
Humanities Computing Unit
Oxford University Computing Services
13 Banbury Road
Oxford OX2 6NN

Series Editors

Marilyn Deegan, Professor of Electronic Library Research, De Montfort University
Christine Mullings, Research Officer, OHC
Michael Fraser, Research Officer, CTI Textual Studies

Editorial Board

Graham Chesters, University of Hull
Peter Denley, Queen Mary and Westfield College, London
Nigel Gardner, University of Ulster
Susan Hockey, Rutgers and Princeton Universities
Willard McCarty, University of Toronto
Nigel McCartney, The British Library
Allen Renear, Brown University
Seamus Ross, The British Academy
Harold Short, King's College, London
Kathryn Sutherland, University of Nottingham

Contents

Introduction

I

For the past two years or so, there has been an explosion in the use of communication by means of electronic technology. Increasingly we find this new communication medium insinuating itself into every area of our life and work: if we are handed a business card it is as likely to contain an e-mail address as a telephone number; television advertisements give a World Wide Web URL as a contact point for a company; we are told (though some of us find it more difficult to believe than others) that it is possible to have sexual relations through the networks; and one research group in Cambridge set up a digital video camera trained on the group coffee machine which allowed them to see if the coffee was ready through their computers without their having to walk into another room. Such is the interest in such mundane information if it is made available through networks that when the group put the camera on their World Wide Web site, they had many thousands of accesses from around the world from others wishing to check on the progress of a pot of coffee in Cambridge.

It is not only electronic communication with which this volume is concerned, but also the delivery of information and scholarship through a variety of electronic media: CD-ROMs and other kinds of storage media as well as networks. And it is not the media themselves we are interested in, but the changes which are wrought in the work we do and the lives we lead through the use of these media. Why, if the ideas we have and the sources we access are essentially the same, do we have the perception that our world is ineluctably different from before? One of the key questions we need to ask ourselves in the face of the new developments concerns the ontology of electronic publications. Most electronic publications are currently available as CD-ROMs (though a few small ones are available on floppy disk). But what exactly is a CD-ROM? Is it a special case of a book, or a special case of a piece of software? Is it content which defines it or is it form? Is, as McLuhan has taught us to ask, the medium the message? A CD-ROM may contain exactly the same materials as a book, but the change of *form*, even without any great change of *content*, means that we are dealing with a very different entity. CD-ROMs are of interest to the same scholars as the books; they may be accessible in the same areas in the library; but if they are made available across networks they can also be used in many other places at the same time. They need other entities to be interposed between themselves and their readers such as hardware, software, interfaces, operating systems, and readers have to be taught how to use them. This is a particularly revolutionary change as publishers and librarians never expected that in selling or providing books, they would have to teach people how to read them.

The questions we were asking at the conferences which generated this volume were concerned with the changes we are seeing in our daily lives through these new and exciting developments in the print culture which, for most of us as academics, constitutes a crucial part of our existence: some scholars are embracing these changes with delight and are helping to mould scholarship into new forms, others are resisting and proclaiming the death knell for the book as we know it. None of the writers in this volume doubts that the book has a future, but equally none is sure that the book will or should be something which is printed on paper.

II

The essays in this volume had their origin in two conferences co-sponsored by the CTI Centre for Textual Studies and the Office for Humanities Communication, Oxford University, and the Centre for English Studies, University of London. The first of these, organized by Andrew Gibson and Noel Heather, and held on 13 January 1995 in London, was entitled 'Theory and Computing Culture' while the second, organized by Marilyn Deegan and held in Oxford on 17 February 1995, was called 'Beyond the Book: Text in the World of Electronic Communication'. Participants came from a wide range of disciplines, but shared an interest in the cultural and political implications of changes brought about by new modes of communication, publication, and discourse in electronic form. The editors felt that the lively dialogue which ensued deserved a wider audience, and a number of those who spoke at the two linked conferences prepared revised versions of their papers with this in mind.

The essays in this volume represent a number of approaches but none is Luddite, demonizing science and technology, though most of the authors express some caution in assessing claims for revolutionary transformation as humans mutate into cyborgs. A common theme in the essays is that some sort of epistemic shift is in progress, prompted and made possible by increased access to and familiarity with electronic technology, and that the new world of the Internet and the electronic archive can be characterized as postmodernist. George Landow in his essay argues that 'the new digital technologies of cultural memory' have far-reaching consequences, and that the implications of the 'shift from physical to digital' have been underestimated. But despite the title of the second conference, few of the speakers felt that contemporary civilization has gone, or in the foreseeable future would go irrevocably 'beyond the book', with the printed book disappearing except as a quaint relic of an outmoded civilization. All the speakers felt that 'computing culture' and 'print culture' were in certain significant respects incompatible, and the conference both registered and sought to analyze a consciousness of cultural dislocation and anxiety characteristic of eras of transition.

A common theme in several of the essays is that the rapid pace of change in electronic technology can be either liberating or oppressive, can perpetuate long-standing injustice or serve to undermine it. Technology is never innocent and a long tradition of literary works, from *Doctor Faustus* to *Frankenstein* and beyond, warns of the dangers as well as suggesting the attractions of the marriage of knowledge and power. Much of the recent publicity about the glories of cyberspace has been generated by commercial considerations: the desire by the manufacturers and promoters of operating systems and communications software to sell as much of their product as possible, to outflank the opposition, open up worldwide markets, and make potential customers feel ashamed if they don't have the newest model. The vast sums of money invested in electronic technology and the enormous profits to be made from its marketing and exploitation make the humanist (or anti-humanist) scholar at his or her wordprocessor a very small player in the game. Nevertheless, as these essays show, the traditional function of the intellectual as gadfly and whistle-blower, rather than being outmoded, is all the more essential as we approach the promises and uncertainties of uncharted cyberspace. To quote Shelley in another great age of expansion, 'we want the creative faculty to imagine what we know ... our calculations have outrun conception; we have eaten more than we can digest. The cultivation of those sciences which have enlarged the limits of the empire of man over the external world has ... proportionally circumscribed those of the internal world; and man, having enslaved the elements, is himself a slave'.[1]

The essays by Kathryn Sutherland, George Landow, Sadie Plant, and John Pickering agree in their conviction that 'electronic technology is challenging our previously held understanding of how knowledge and information are organized' in Western culture, but differ in their attitudes toward the information revolution and its relationship to traditional scholarship in the humanities. Kathryn Sutherland's essay approaches the frontier of cyberspace with some caution, emphasizing the problematical aspects of the relocation of the sites of knowledge brought about by access to 'instantly accessible information' through electronic technology: 'will new knowledge be determined by our ability to locate, transfer, and appropriate at an ever faster rate expert entries from larger sets of information that we no longer need to understand?' The movement from 'expert-led' to 'user-led' organization and delivery of knowledge may challenge 'inherited structures' of learning and the idea of an overarching fundamental truth independent of 'the contingent strategies for its perception' but, as Sutherland suggests, these new structures of learning are no less ideologically and economically determined than the old ones. For Sutherland, the attack on 'the privileged category of authority itself' is the most significant intellectual consequence of the information revolution.

Yet her essay raises the possibility that authority has not been decentred so much as made invisible, and that claims for the 'democratization of information' may be self-delusion. George Landow in his essay directs a salutary irony toward the conventional humanist fear of technology as a demonized Other and its concomitant sentimentalizing of the 'ideal utopian book' as precious, endangered object. As Landow points out, the printed book itself is a product of technology, with a concrete material existence, rather than inhabiting an imagined ideal realm free of contamination: 'we have to remind ourselves that if, how, and whenever we move beyond the book, that movement will not embody a movement from something natural or human to something artificial'. Indeed, since most of the books we actually encounter are 'ill-designed, fragile, short-lived objects', and since a digitally stored text can be reproduced 'an indefinite number of times' without wear and tear, it can be argued that the electronic text, which can be called up in a moment and made to disappear at the touch of a key, is both more permanent and less permanent than the printed text. Everything one reads on a computer screen is *virtual*, reinforcing the principle that the text and 'its physical instantiation' are distinct (or conversely, the poststructuralist principle that there can be no 'finished corpus of writing' but only a 'differential network' of traces, some fading more rapidly than others).

Sadie Plant, like Landow, sees both the 'greater ease of manipulability and reconfigurability' of texts and 'connecting computers together in networks' as defining the transition between print culture and a new realm holding forth great promise. Like Sutherland, Plant in her essay emphasizes the ways in which digitization and its consequences challenge the assumptions, common in traditional humanist scholarship, that 'man is the centre of the world and the point of its investigations', but Plant, rather than registering a 'sense of cultural dislocation', presents the advent of the 'posthumanities', made possible by new technology, as wholly liberatory. From the perspective of a radical cultural studies, as argued here, 'the top-down imposition of knowledge', the 'techniques of policing' by which a dominant ideology maintains hegemony, are rendered ineffective by the disruptive potential of 'hypertext systems which function regardless of canons and set texts', systems which function 'in precisely the way that synapses function in the human brain'. John Pickering, like Plant, examines the political and pedagogical implications of the 'shift from isolated linear texts to interconnected web-like hypertexts', but his approach is sceptical rather than celebratory. While Pickering sees 'the explosive growth of information technology' as an incontrovertible fact, a product of a postmodern 'cultural condition ... of fluid and mobile signification', he denies that this epistemic shift involves the supplanting of one cultural model by another, but rather presents it as an 'encounter' to be negotiated. Though inevitably 'hypermedia will bring new tools and practices to certain communities of practice', the book will remain as an instrument of discourse particularly well adapted to 'a narrative or a sustained critical argument'. Changes in pedagogical practice made possible by electronic technology, Pickering reminds us, can have both positive and negative consequences: on the one hand, 'automated searches of databases using sophisticated tools', on the other, the likelihood that 'more computers mean fewer teachers' and that access to these valuable resources will be determined wholly by ability to pay.

Michael Allen in his essay considers some of the far-reaching consequences of technological advances in multimedia in one intellectual discipline, Film Studies, showing how the advent of new technology will inevitably change 'the way Film Studies writing will be conceived', and will no less profoundly affect teaching practice. Like Pickering, Allen sees problems along with opportunities, in access to rare archives (whose custodians may wish to protect their treasures), in the degraded quality of image and sound which the computer can reproduce, and in the possibility that 'the available technology can partially determine' what is to be studied and how it is to be studied. Yet for Allen 'the immediate, direct, and precisely controllable quotation of the film text itself', made possible by multimedia technology, is a development which transforms the discipline. Laura Chernaik, in considering the imagined world of the Science Fiction writer Samuel Delany in which information technology has developed instruments with a seemingly limitless capacity to control and to liberate, presents Delany as a 'deeply political' writer whose fictive world is both radically different from and depressingly similar to our own. The powerful 'Web', an instrument of surveillance and control throughout the multiplanetary universe of Delany's novel, produces and distributes information: its sinister aspects, which can be seen as an extrapolation from our contemporary transnational economy, are counterbalanced in the novel, as Chernaik's essay shows, by the capacity it gives, in enabling access to knowledge, to free those who were once slaves. Ignorance is slavery, freedom (in the action of the novel made possible by an IT prosthesis provided by the Web, making one of the central characters literally a cyborg) is defined as the ability to process new information and to judge or question.

Where the essay on Samuel Delany's work shows how the traditional form of the printed book can, by sustained argument or narrative, help us to understand the transformations which electronic technology make possible, Andrew Gibson's 'Interactive Fiction and Narrative Space' treats the possible impact of available computing technology on narrative itself. This essay examines the problematical relationship of computerized interactive fiction, in the form of adventure games and hypertext narratives, with a narrative theory which has, as Gibson argues, failed to take into account newer forms of fiction which exist 'beyond the book'. Gibson uses the 'forking paths' and multiple, heterogeneous narrative space characteristic of IF to challenge and deconstruct the 'geometric' and determinist assumptions of narratology, presenting IF as 'the postmodern mode of narrative *par excellence*'. Nina Wakeford's 'Sexualized Bodies in Cyberspace', which shares the view of several essays in the volume that the conventional distinctions between 'natural' and 'technological' are ideological impositions, considers some of the problematical aspects of 'computer mediated communications within the more unstable category of cyberspace'. One of the claims frequently advanced for the virtual reality of the Internet is that, as Howard Rheingold puts it, 'people in virtual communities do just about everything people do in real life, but we leave our bodies behind'[2]—in other words, that the experience of entering cyberspace can be entirely liberatory, enabling a 'total refashioning of the self', free from physical or societal constraints. Wakeford's witty and disturbing essay suggests that despite these impressive claims, the dominant values of society are more often than not simply replicated in cyberspace: in practice, as she shows, cyberspace is gendered, marginalizing those participants who would seek to maintain a stance outside an ideological norm of 'virtual heterosexual interaction' where all men are seen as predators and all women as prey. The realm of cyberspace, rather than providing an ideal space for free play, may simply provide a differently configured apparatus of social control.

III

If this volume of essays demonstrates one thing, it is that the new technology is no longer entirely the province of pragmatists and realists. It has become a concern for theory, too; the difficulty being that the technology is not merely an object of theoretical interest, but threatens to transform the very theory it encounters. A recurrent concern in the essays in the volume is the question of the relationship between the new technology and the concept of postmodernity. In one way or another, contemporary theory has given expression to a widespread sense that a transformation of thought is taking place within our culture. Postmodernity is partly to be understood as the name we give to the epistemic shift we take to be under way in our times. The shift in question, however, is distinctive in that it has not manifested itself as a clean and decisive break with the past. It rather declares the impossibility of any such break, of any final *Uberwindung* or 'overcoming' of the past, to use the Heideggerian term employed recently by Gianni Vattimo.[3] In this account of it, postmodernity is thus marked by a paradoxical or—as Vattimo has it—a 'weakened' thought that sees the necessity of a leap beyond fixed horizons that it nonetheless cannot make. In *The Gay Science*, Nietzsche called this 'continuing to dream, knowing that we are dreaming'.[4] For Vattimo, Lyotard and others, however, postmodern culture has equally been marked by the explosion of the new media, including those made available by the new technology. In Vattimo's terms, postmodern culture is the product of 'a society of generalized communication' (*TS*, p. 45). What, then, is the relation of the new media to the epistemic shift just described? How far are the new media products or reflections of that shift? Might they not actually be producing it themselves? Might they not transform it, or transform our understanding of it? Alternatively, might they not expose epistemic shift and postmodernity alike as illusions, born of a reluctance to accept the inexorable advance of technology as knowledge?

Two contrasting views of the meaning of the new technology might be characterized as the modern and the postmodern. Both are much in evidence in the present volume, sometimes co-existing in a single essay. Each brings with it a distinctive conception of the text and a distinctive politics. The 'modern' reading of the new technology is expressed in the last of the list of questions above. It is a progressive reading. Whether explicitly or not, it understands the new technology as an extension if not a culmination of the Enlightenment project. Ours becomes the age of the triumph of modernity in techno-science. In the 'modern' account of it, the new technology becomes a means to greater *transparency*: improved understanding, better and more extensive knowledge, clearer and more plausible representations. The new technology therefore does not usher in a transformation of knowledge or thought. It is rather another stage in our emancipation or, at least, in the growth of our power over our world. This is new technology as it has recently been espoused by Tony Blair and New Labour, technology as confident modernization. As far as textual studies are concerned, from the 'modern' perspective, the new technology offers us formidable and exciting new resources. But they are resources which, if they empower us in new ways, are nonetheless to be harnessed to familiar endeavours and tied to established modes of cognition. In this version of it, for instance, hypertext is not a new form of textuality which transforms the texts that serve as its raw material. It is a better and more effective presentation of textuality itself. Equally, in political terms, in the modern reading, the new technology means better and more democratic social relations. Apel's view of the new media provides one example of this. More information is being circulated. We move progressively towards a 'community of unlimited communication'.5 In this community, what Apel calls 'logical socialism' will be realized as society becomes ever more transparent to itself. The major question, then, is how to ensure that all members of the community may participate equally in communication. The possibility and desirability of such participation, however, is not in doubt.

The postmodern account of the new media, however—as exemplified in Vattimo's work—is very different. It suggests, as the modern account does not, that we must think of the effects of the new technology in paradoxical terms. Paradoxically, says Vattimo, the more sophisticated the means of knowledge, understanding, representation and comm-unication that we develop, the more powerfully they come to subvert the very possibility of unitary knowledge and representation themselves:

> In general, the intense development of the human sciences and the intensification of social communication do not seem to produce a growth in the self-transparency of society ... From this perspective, the idea of a world history [for instance] is revealed for what it always has been, namely a reduction of the train of human events from a single perspective which is in each case a function of domination, whether class-based or colonial, etc. Something of the kind probably holds for the ideal of society's self-transparency as well. Although it only works from the point of view of a central subject, such a subject becomes ever more unthinkable with each advance in the technology that should make its realization 'possible'.
> (*TS*, p. 24)

Instead of making postmodern society more transparent, the new media are making it more complex and even chaotic. They are shattering the unilinear structures and centralized perspectives, for example, on which an established knowledge depended. They are producing a range of dispersed and incommensurable centres of knowledge, communication, and representation. In the process, the very possibility of sustaining a faith in a unitary reality principle dissolves. What we might once have called the 'reality of the world' has now become the context for a multiplicity of 'fablings', in the sense in which Nietzsche meant the latter term when, in *Twilight of the Idols*, he proclaimed that the true world had become a fable. The new media and the new technology are engaged in the generation, proliferation and diversification of such 'fables'. As regards textuality, the postmodern view asserts the constitutive difference of the electronic text. For the postmodernist, the electronic text is diffuse, open, multiple, without a determining sequence. It gives virtuality and actuality equivalent status, and makes possible the transgression of established textual boundaries, including those presumed to exist between 'high' and 'low' cultural forms. Like the Net itself, hypertext is a decentred network of dispersed items or activities which cannot be brought back to the terms of the old, unitary structures. On the other hand, as regards the politics of the new media (including the 'politics of cyberspace'), Vattimo argues that the liberating power of the media should be conceived of less in terms of emancipation than *disorientation*. Disorientation is 'the liberation of differences, of local elements, of what could generally be called dialect'. Here,

> the world of generalized communication explodes like a multiplicity of 'local' rationalities—ethnic, sexual, religious, cultural or aesthetic minorities—that finally speak up for themselves. They are no longer repressed and cowed into silence by the idea of a single true form of

humanity that must be realized irrespective of particularity and individual finitude, transience and contingency. (*TS*, p. 9)

It is in terms of difference that we must think today, in ever smaller, more subtle and precise forms. For Vattimo (as, we might add, for others, notably Lyotard),[6] Apel's 'community of unlimited communication' is predicated on an assumption of communicative foundations, and will necessarily mean the containment of difference. In the new media and the new technology, on the other hand, lie the seeds of a genuinely pluralistic 'ethic of interpretations' and, ultimately, of a democratic 'heterotopia'.[7]

As a whole, this collection of essays does not choose between the modern and postmodern readings of the new technology (though individual essays may do so). There is rather a kind of shifting back and forth between the two, throughout the book, of a kind which Vattimo refers to as 'oscillation' and sees as one expression of the experience of postmodernity. 'Oscillation' is a movement between familiar and possible worlds, belonging and disorientation. The concept implies that, for us, at least, the issue of the modern and postmodern views of the new technology is an undecidable one. To return to a point made earlier: paradoxically, again, here as in other respects, postmodernity is unable to dispense with, transcend, or 'overcome' modernity. Rather, the two cohabit in a relationship that is neither exactly amiable nor conflictual, but one precisely of oscillation. The same relationship persists in this book. One aspect of the postmodern condition, then, would be that it is neither singular nor self-consistent nor 'covered' by its nomination. As we have so often been told, it both comes after and is contemporary with modernity. Nothing could better demonstrate this than the growing diversity of our accounts of the new technology and its effects. Hence the need for a book of this kind. At the very least, it surely serves as a precise registration of a historically specific question; a question to which, for the present, there is no clear and unambiguous answer.

Notes

1. Percy Bysshe Shelley, *The Defence of Poetry* in *Shelley's Prose*, ed. David Lee Clark (New York: New Amsterdam Books, 1988), 293.
2. Howard Rheingold, *The Virtual Community: Homesteading on the Electronic Frontier* (Reading: Addison-Wesley, 1993), 3.
3. Gianni Vattimo, *The End of Modernity: Nihilism and Hermeneutic in Post-Modern Culture*, translated with an introduction by Jon R. Snyder (Oxford: Polity Press, 1988).
4. Quoted in Vattimo, *The Transparent Society*, translated by David Webb (Oxford: Polity Press, 1992), 9.
5. See Karl Otto Apel, *Transformation der Philosophie*, 2 vols. (Frankfurt am Main: Suhrkamp Verlag, 1973).

6. See in particular Jean-François Lyotard, *The Differend: Phrases in Dispute*, translated by Georges van den Abbeele (Manchester: Manchester University Press, 1988), passim.

7. See in particular Vattimo, 'From Utopia to Heterotopia', *The Transparent Society*, 62-75.

Looking and Knowing: Textual Encounters of a Postponed Kind

Kathryn Sutherland
Department of English
University of Nottingham

This essay is concerned with the use of computers and other devices of the new technology to present the work of scholars in the humanities. Superficially, at least, it explores a conjunction of opposites: on the one side, there is the information revolution, anarchic, global, culturally levelling, and largely uncritical in its methods; on the other, there is scholarship, selective, judgemental, and exclusive in its cultural priorities. But through the conjunction what we know and how we know it are changed. Electronic technology is challenging our previously held understanding of how knowledge and information are organized and, to use a potent word, how they are legitimated in the Western world. The argument that follows is developed in terms of two conditioning assumptions—one is my conviction of the need to harness the intellectual caution of humanist scholars towards the new electronic technology as the necessary critical context within which that technology should be deployed, and the other is the assumption that this new technology is not itself a *thing* in the way that Literature or History, however broadly or narrowly, canonically or extra-canonically we define them, are *things*. However, though not a thing as such, electronic technology and humanities computing, through which many of its features and procedures are disseminated to humanist scholars, do provide a way of organizing that brings its own inflections to what is organized, inflections which are ideologically and economically defining and defined. My argument also assumes that in representing a selection of what is known, electronic technology represents a society to itself.

The immediate society that concerns me is the society of scholars, but also scholars as a subset of the larger society. For the scholar's relation to the electronic environment quite properly and inevitably replicates aspects of a general shift in our systems of knowing and acquiring knowledge. This larger shift is both technological and non-technological. It is, speaking generally, an aspect of the postmodern condition. And this is what concerns me here, the computing culture as an aspect of postmodern society, and the computer as disseminator of the postmodern agenda in scholarship. As scholars in the humanities, we need to have views on this: we need to consider how the electronic environment reconfigures what is already known and, beyond this, what new ways of knowing it makes available and even privileges. In other words, though not a thing, the new electronic technology has to be seen as more than technical support and services, however locally specific or globally generalized, for the humanities. Its use needs to develop in terms of a reflective understanding of its practices, and in terms of a critically interventionist understanding of the powers and limits of a technology which will not go away. In an obvious sense my argument grows from and is indebted to Jean-Franc̜ois Lyotard's report on the state of knowledge in the western world, *The Postmodern Condition*.[1]

It is already clear that the computer is revolutionizing the way we use and understand *text* (strings of written characters) and *texts* (those objects whose primary function is to relay written information). What interests me as a literary critic is the computer's capacity to produce a particularly intense postmodern experience—what I would call textual encounters of a postponed kind; that is, the computer's capacity to combine textual immediacy with certain kinds of textual deferral. By this I do not simply mean to draw attention to the electronic accessing of virtual copies of works whose existence is premised on their real absence, but to a more complicated textual deferral whereby the computer's liberation of text from previously fixed boundaries calls into question not just the desirability but the possibility of determining textual limits, to the extent that the identity of text itself is displaced by its own excess.

In Europe since the Middle Ages (and long before if we include a manuscript tradition) the codex, the book composed of quires (as distinct from the *volumen* or roll) has been the dominant means, our most powerful tool, for developing, storing, and distributing textual information. Over centuries, it has evolved specialized protocols and formulas, search engines and tools for navigation (contents pages, glossaries, indices, footnotes, critical apparatus of various kinds), all designed to organize, retrieve, and discriminate between the complexly related or distinct kinds of information held within text. Yet there are problems, highlighted by the case of the literary work: in their presentation of knowledge books are profoundly inauthentic.

The inauthenticity can be stated like this: painters paint pictures; sculptors carve statues; but authors do not author books. Books are material objects which present one authority by means of another. There is a complicated distribution of authority within the world of print communication which makes reproduction and substitution the almost irresistible conditions of its authority. The distinction is a simple one—in a sense, too simple, for of course all works of art can be viewed as the impure mediations of an original intention; but in the case of the literary work this mediation is particularly sophisticated. The so-called 'electronic' book is a meta-book whose capacity to reorganize at a higher level the information and scientific tools within a book provides its own comment on bookish structures. This potential makes the electronic book both more and less bookish. Something of this 'less' and this 'more' is expressed in the term hypertext, where the prefix 'hyper' denotes 'beyond' and 'excess' (though not all electronic books are hypertext). Since its organization is dependent on electronic links and not sequenced pagination, the electronic book makes available structured collections of textual and non-textual information in multiple relation one to another; there is no necessarily determining sequence in which the parts are related. Ordering is multi-sequential; and so the electronic book frees the page-bound book from its codex-defined limitations. Of course, one might make the counter-assertion that a well-structured index and the fingers of one hand can often provide a satisfactory form of the same function. But it can be further asserted that the extra fluidity and non-integrity of information in the electronic book mimics the mind's associative grouping and re-grouping of ideas and materials. This mind might be the author's or the reader's. In this sense, the electronic book is a powerful non-prioritizing modeller rather than a finite arrangement of information.

The electronic book appears to make two contradictory promises to its users (whether authors or readers). It promises immediate access. This might be quicker availability of subsets of information—the kernel of an argument or the specific requirements of a particular literary or linguistic search (all the instances of a word or theme in a book or a body of materials)—or it might be a closer approximation, in the case of certain literary works, to a more seemingly authentic representation of authorial intention. To take two examples from my own research field, Romantic English Literature, this seeming authenticity might be represented by an electronic image and word archive of the engraver-poet William Blake's *Songs of Innocence and Experience*, one which stores images of all the extant copies of his uniquely customized plates rather than reducing them to a single and distorting definitive set as any book-bound edition would have to do; or it might be a multi-text edition of William Wordsworth's four-version epic *The Prelude*, where split-screen facilities would enhance the interconnections between versions and emphasize the organic, emergent nature of both work and poetic subject. In codex-based scholarly editions, these works are in constant conflict with their physical forms, as the 'reading text' of the definitive Cornell edition of *The Prelude* shows, where a multi-layered critical apparatus betrays the indecisive and shifting state of what appears to be a fixed text.[2]

But if it promises immediate access, even enhanced authenticity, the electronic environment also promises seemingly endless deferral—of choice, preference, exclusion—and this is the other half of the contradiction. All those judgements which dog the editor of literary works (best text, copytext, final intention, and so on), and which are endemic to the book, can be postponed indefinitely within the electronic environment. Where the satisfactions of book-bound communication are determined by closure—selecting the crucial information, the decisive examples, discarding the extraneous—those of the electronic medium are open-ended. The one offers the pleasurable illusion of completeness, the other holds out the promise of more, a never-to-be satisfied craving. In this sense, the computer models that deregulation of desire which is at the heart of most commercially-driven definitions of freedom in late twentieth-century western society. In place of selection and the need or even art of choosing, the computer reinstates a sense of the nearly infinite range of possibilities which exists in life. Computerized information is premised on excess and on the permeability and transgression of boundaries.

The computer, then, denotes more power—apparently to readers, and perhaps also to the authors and editors of books. In doing so, it models that redistribution of controls and resetting of perspectives which characterize postmodernism as a movement or tendency within late twentieth-century culture. The postmodern direction is, or is claimed to be, from essentialism to pluralism; from analysis, definition, and certainty to ironic juxtaposition and uncertainty; from the mechanical, specialist, and restricted to the organic, distributed, and interconnected. In terms of texts, the postmodern reader is a participating user for whom the electronic environment provides training in search skills to substitute for memory, opportunities for discovery instead of instruction, and processes in place of outcomes.

As tool of the postmodern scholarly agenda, the computer enters the debate with Enlightenment and post-Enlightenment constructions of knowledge. Postmodernism denies the possibility of a fundamental reason or core of truth that can be discovered and that exists separately from the contingent strategies for its perception. Radically removed alike from the rational metanarratives and enclosed systems of Enlightenment thought and from the alternative fundamental subjectivities of the Romantic Imagination, postmodern thinking admits neither an external, impartial perspective nor a totalizing subjectivity. There can be no overarching constructions of meaning, only the uncomfortable knowledge of the ironic coexistence of what can neither be reduced (down) to nor theorized (up) to a unified truth. Postmodern explanations of meaning emphasize instability, indeterminacy, the priority (as in Derrida, Lacan, and the later Barthes) of signifier over signified. The shifting criteria of persuasion, performance, and play replace a search for truth, while, at a textual level, origin or source of meaning as embodied in the concept of a primary textual witness gives way to the open-ended, non-prioritized exchanges of the intertextual. The shift implies a loosening, too, of the moral imperatives of former expert systems of instruction, as the now fashionable computer-born term 'edutainment' suggests. As in postmodernism itself, the division between high and low culture is consciously blurred. What the computer and electronic space are facilitating is the postmodern reconception of our inherited structures for knowing, which in scholarship are represented by the discipline-based, professionalized, scientific methods advanced since the nineteenth century. What is replacing them is a promiscuous merging or collision of previously compartmentalized categories of knowledge, an impermanent customization of information which presents itself as user- rather than expert-led.

Within the discipline of Textual Studies, the advent of the new technology has led quickly to an interesting substitution of terms: of 'archive' for 'edition' and of 'text' for 'work'. Printed books come to us in editions, whether or not those editions are mediated through a critical editor, as with dead authors and works, like those of Greek and Roman classical writers, for which no autograph manuscripts survive and no copies collated with an original. Traditionally, the business of the scholarly editor was to produce a text as close as possible to an original intention, whether that is understood as a substitution for a lost manuscript witness or as a simulation of the ideal purpose of a particular author. Whichever condition applied, the assumption was that the editor worked objectively and according to precise scientific principles. A recent shift, the result of the theorizing of editing, has been to reassess this objectivity and to admit that the scholarly editor engages in selection and discrimination—that editorial judgements are finally subjective, even when those judgements are presented as the result of a trained understanding or intuition of what would have been an author's or original's 'intention' (itself a concept which is now called into question).[3] Unlike the edition, however, the archive denies any provisional or mediated status. It denies individual agency in its assembly; it implies a neutral, unmediated storehouse of facts/data awaiting the reader or user who then her-/ himself takes on the role of editor, choosing to define connections between documents in a variety of temporary ways. What is rendered fluid (potentially if not actually in the electronic archive) is the fixed, prioritizing relation which characterizes the book-bound edition—the relation of 'definitive text', 'copytext', 'ideal text', 'reading text', 'Ur text', and so on.

Jerome McGann, a textual critic and theoretician with long experience of traditional editing, refers to his Dante Gabriel Rossetti hypermedia database as an 'archive'.[4] It is an archive which potentially holds within it several critical editions. Such a rearrangement of priorities—the privileging of the 'raw' over the 'cooked' ingredients of editing—appears endemic to the electronic status of information and points to the current competing desires to view the computer environment as both subjectifier and objectifier—partial (by virtue of its rapid powers of selection) and impartial (by virtue of its totalizing storage capacity). As postmodern tool, the computer problematizes notions of authority differently from the book: within the electronic environment prescribed authority is both less visible (but no less determining) and more apparently within the control of each individual user.

Two opposed theoretic movements have anticipated some of the thinking that accompanies electronic textuality, though, interestingly, few of their exponents have so far acted upon the connection. Deconstruction looks for insights in textual gaps and contradictions, in subtexts which subvert ostensible meaning. Coherence, argues the deconstructionist critic, may be merely a matter of co-optation; there is value in incoherence.

Theories of the unconscious and notions of textual playfulness are harnessed to deconstruct text and de-authorize authority. Deconstruction relates closely to some of the uses of electronic hypertext. But hypertext also offers intriguing possibilities for recovering the extra-canonical and enabling contextual environments of works—the possibility of simulating particular historical editions, virtual copies of socially embedding materials—and their extra-textual dimensions—images, sound. McGann's Rossetti Archive, for instance, is planned as a multi-media, hypertextual variorum bundle that will put into practice his long-held commitment to fixing the entire socio-history of the work from its originary moments of production through all its subsequent reproductive adventures.

Operating though they do as theoretic oppositions, the deconstructive and the sociological approach nevertheless share a project to dissipate authorial integrity (including the integrity of the human 'subject') in favour of a plurality of meanings and categories, a dispersed and decentred network of activities. What is under attack is the privileged category of authority itself. By extension, in the electronic book there are texts but not works. 'Work' is a manifestly relegated term, and this is interesting; for while we celebrate the computer's capacity for textual acquisition, we do not feel tempted to extend that to include the conceptual entity of work. The work is that mysterious (authored?) product to which the various texts witness, implying a value apart from and irreducible to any single representation as text. The computer is a multi-text facilitator. Given sufficient power, it can store and customize at command a variety of texts each with its particular status or claim to authority. For example, the joint Oxford-Sheffield Universities' *Canterbury Tales Project* intends to make available, over a ten-year period and in computer-readable form, transcripts, images, collations, and analyses of all eighty-four extant manuscripts and four pre-1500 printed editions of Chaucer's *Canterbury Tales*. It will simply overshadow every previous edition of Chaucer, transforming the edition itself into an analogue computer, capable of reconstituting past and future texts.

These are the texts, but where is Chaucer's work? Is it that the 'work', which used not to be precisely equatable with its textual transmissions, however many of them we stored, now exists in a different and demoted cognitive space? Work denotes both labour and creation and suggests human agency ('the product of the operation or labour of a person or other agent; creation', *OED*, sense 1). Work carries, too, in this context, certain moral attributes ('work of art connoting high artistic quality', *OED*, sense 6). More generally, in the classical, pre-computer tradition, work/labour denotes virtue. What have been displaced in the computer revolution are these concepts of 'labour' and 'virtue', and with them human identity through labour. The shift is already apparent in both deconstruction and sociological criticism. According to Derrida's famous early definition, a text-work relationship is rendered tenuous because text denies boundaries:

'text [is]—no longer a finished corpus of writing, some content enclosed in a book or its margins, but a differential network, a fabric of traces referring endlessly to something other than itself, to other differential traces.'5 Ten years later, against G. Thomas Tanselle's idealistic distinction—'[a] work is not fully knowable through any of its written manifestations . . . the documentary texts of all literary . . . works [are] but imperfect guides to the works they attempt to transmit'—Jerome McGann declares that the text is the only manifestation of the work.[6]

Over the last five years, the most glibly reiterated claim for the electronic environment has been that *per se* it initiates a redistribution of cultural controls. Over-employed and under-defined terms, like 'democratization of information' and 'decentring of authority', typically accompany descriptions of hypertext projects.[7] At some level, the truth-value of such assertions is perhaps irrelevant; what is of interest is the need to make them. As Walter Ong implies, in his distinctions between orality, literacy, and secondary orality (which includes electronic technologies), there is a quality of nostalgia endemic to the programmatic group identifications and planned spontaneity of the highly self-conscious secondary orality:

This new orality has striking resemblances to the old in its participatory mystique, its fostering of a communal sense, its concentration on the present moment, and even its use of formulas. But it is essentially a more deliberate and self-conscious orality . . . Unlike members of a primary oral culture, who are turned outward because they have had little occasion to turn inward, we are turned outward because we have turned inward. In a like vein, where primary orality promotes spontaneity because the analytic reflectiveness implemented by writing is unavailable, secondary orality promotes spontaneity because through analytic reflection we have decided that spontaneity is a good thing. We plan our happenings carefully to be sure that they are thoroughly spontaneous.[8]

While the relevance of Ong's remarks to telephone, radio, and television are obvious, no less pertinent is their application to the disposability, the reconfiguration, and the key-stroke immediacy of electronic scholarship. Like postmodernity itself, computer scholarship operates within a culture of fragmentary sensations, shifting simulacra, and wistful nostalgia. The nostalgia factor within computer culture should not be underestimated; like the postmodern substitution of text for work, the immediacy and high informational tolerance of the electronic environment feed a yearning for wholeness and an illusion of comprehensiveness which its very procedures of excess and substitution postpone and call into doubt.

Despite the hype, we all know that in any realization open-endedness and democracy of information are the *unrealized* promises proffered by the limited entries in a database; diffused or concealed controls, in the form of selected, edited, even pre-linked data blocks, do not constitute an absence of authority. Envisaging his Rossetti Archive as an exhaustive textual space containing 'all the original documents that the scholar needs or wants',[9] McGann also proposes a managing board of scholars to maintain and select data, a possible list of subscribers, and even selective entry of readers to various levels of the Archive. We do not yet think sufficiently critically about our practices in relation to either the so-called totalizing or the selective capacities of the electronic environment. What are the conditions and limits within which these functions operate? whose totality do they represent? whose selection? and by virtue of what agenda, what knowledge?

Psychologists can perhaps explain why it is that the glamour of the screen absorbs the user into the illusion of a total environment, an artfully homogenized representation of meaning; and why it is that material processed and displayed electronically at one and the same time sets up expectations of bias-free communication, completeness of information, and personal control. Writing in 1989, William Paulson anticipated a time when written works would cease to exist under the conditions of their production and be realized only as an 'infinitely reproducible *musée imaginaire*'.[10] Techniques for reproduction, forms of reproduction, and modes of reading are complexly related. There is the possibility at least that in its screen display of instantly accessible information, the computer will deliver knowledge as spectacle—knowing as looking. Herein lies the greatest challenge posed by the electronic environment to those expert divisions of knowledge established in the west in the course of the nineteenth century as the best means of advancing learning in an industrial society. If the computer merely displays knowledge to a post-productive society, what might this imply about our mechanisms for generating new (as opposed to retrieving and redeploying old) expert knowledge? How real is the danger that the scholar-worker, whose origins lie in a nineteenth-century conception of learning as heroic endeavour, will be transformed into the scholar-technician? Without the underpinning of a certain kind of labour, will new knowledge be determined by our ability to locate, transfer, and appropriate at an ever faster rate expert entries from larger sets of information that we no longer need to understand?

The relegation or invisibility of labour within the electronic environment finds its exemplification in what is both a cultural and a linguistic shift, from virtuous to virtual knowing. For Thomas Carlyle in 1840, at the start of the professionalization of literature, the man of letters (a term including writer, critic, and scholar) was the modern manifestation of the hero and as such a shaper of 'Universal History', which is 'the history of what man has accomplished in this world . . . the History of the Great Men who have worked here.'[11] Carlyle was confident that the man of letters 'may be expected to continue, as one of the main forms of Heroism for all future ages.'[12] Determined by the conventions of classical heroism, the 'virtue' of the man of letters includes both moral excellence and manliness as strength. These constitute the basis for his claim to social guardianship. While the intervening century and a half has seen the reinterpretation of such literary and scholarly virtue in less extreme and more circumspect terms, nevertheless a faded heroic recognition long remained as tribute to the agonistic struggles which mark the attainment and exclusivity of professional status in the world of letters.

'Virtue' and 'virtual' share a root in Latin *virtus*, 'strength', but the adjective implies a displacement of properties included in the abstract noun ('virtue', 'a particular moral excellence', *OED*, sense 3; 'virtu', 'vertu', 'the distinctive qualities inherent in a thing or person', *OED*, Supplement, Add: 4; 'virtual', 'that is so in essence or effect although not formally or actually; admitting of being called by the name so far as the effect or result is concerned', *OED*, sense 3). Semantically the shift is from 'good' to 'almost as good as'; but in terms of what we know and how we know it, it may include an even greater shift. (A comparable and already more accommodated transference can be discerned in the substitution of photocopying for reading, where the *effect* of electronic [passive] copying readily replaces in many instances the *activity* of reading.) Considered from another angle, might the computer's transformation of the labour of learning into the seductive but less virtuous act ('virtue', 'the possession or display of manly qualities', *OED*, sense 6) of merely looking come to denote the same feminization of endeavour (by which I mean cultural disempowerment) it traditionally has done?

The beginnings of a mass print culture in the late eighteenth century witnessed a battle over the meaning (nature and limits) of reading itself. In some quarters, the circulating library, as it was called, and its chief commodity, the novel, were heralded as inaugurating a new demo-cratization of knowledge. As its name implies, the novel was at this time still a relatively new form whose protocols were as yet emergent and unstable. The novel represented a dissemination of knowledge driven by popular market forces rather than by elite ideological purposes. Novels purported to be comprehensive pictures of society, democratic and democratizing in their accessibility, in their non-classical form and subject-matter, and in their blurring of divisions between high and low life. To some critics, novels even appeared to celebrate the anarchic potential of subjective experience and therefore to challenge centralized authority; while to others, novels represented the non-virtuous, idle absorption of pre-packaged experience: it required less effort to read novels than other literary forms, and their totalizing perspectives deprived the reader of external points of view on their practices. Finally, novels were distributed through borrowing and vending outlets whose mechanisms were assumed (by critics and enthusiasts alike) to simulate the circulatory systems of other aspects of society and of human existence—the circulation of money through the public sector and of blood through the body, for example. The circulating library's networks were seen to be pervasive.

Fig. 1. Beauty in Search of Knowledge *(artist unknown, 1782)*

Two statements from the period suggest the determining power of the circulating library. One is provided by an engraving of 1782, artist unknown, entitled 'Beauty in Search of Knowledge' (Fig. 1) and the other by the social critic and philosopher Samuel Taylor Coleridge, writing in 1817. The conjunction, in the engraving, is of a fashionable female figure and the circulating library's shop-window display of texts and images before which she stands as purchaser or borrower, book in hand, not in fact reading but gazing out, like the open commodities behind her, at the implied reader. This conjunction sends some powerful signals and poses some interesting questions. Presumably the woman herself is beauty in search of knowledge, and if this is so, is the inference to be drawn that under these conditions knowledge will be more widely available? or a trouble-free attainment? or that under these conditions knowledge will be marginalized—as feminine, as leisure activity, as frivolous? And what are *these* conditions—the commodification of learning? the ascendancy of entertainment over instruction? the democracy of knowledge? What is clear is that here gender describes the relation between knowledge and its circulation. The female figure bisects the spectacle of knowledge, her display imposing itself between the outer spectator and the window exhibition. How we interpret the female figure's relation to knowledge—as representative of civilized leisure or of (too) easy consumption—may depend on the gendered perspective of the reader.

Coleridge's verdict on 'the devotees of the circulating libraries' is far less equivocal:

> I dare not compliment their *pass-time*, or rather *kill-time*, with the name of *reading*. Call it rather a sort of beggarly day-dreaming, during which the mind of the dreamer furnishes for itself nothing but laziness and a little mawkish sensibility; while the whole *materiel* and imagery of the doze is supplied *ab extra* by a sort of mental *camera obscura* manufactured at the printing office, which *pro tempore* fixes, reflects and transmits the moving phantasms of one man's delirium, so as to people the barrenness of an hundred other brains afflicted with the same trance or suspension of all common sense and all definite purpose.[13]

His fear is that the networks of the circulating library will actually destroy the habit of active reading, and he locates this destruction in a new writer-work-reader relation which the library inaugurates. Implied in its methods of dissemination (its mass distribution and its prescriptive levelling of information) is the library's substitution of a deadening inertia for a lively engagement with knowledge. This inertia is the consequence of both excess and lack—a continuous supply of signals which overruns, exhausts, and finally impoverishes the mind of the recipient who is her-/ himself no more than an effect of the same commodified and technologized social order. From this bleak context, Coleridge proposed redemption by an active, individual (and selective) self-constitution as reader.

The analogy I am suggesting between this earlier information revolution and our own is formal—their sense of cultural dislocation is distinct from but comparable to our own—nor am I attempting to absorb their alienness as a prelude to or sign of our own self-estrangement in a sign-saturated universe. The earlier crisis can, however, make more visible our own and help formulate, though on different terms, the problem if not its solution. New methods, new protocols and forms of assembling knowledge and of learning, are inevitably occasions for cultural reassessment and anxiety. How do we know what we know when we relocate the site of knowledge? and how does what we know relate to what we used to know or believed that we knew? As yet we have scarcely begun to consider the status of authority and knowledge as shaped by the new electronic technologies. As scholars and critics we need to be involved in these debates.

Notes

1. Jean-François Lyotard, *The Postmodern Condition: A Report on Knowledge* (English translation, Manchester: Manchester University Press, 1984).
2. Beginning in July 1995, a hypermedia Blake archive, supported by the Getty Grant Fund and the University of Virginia's Institute for Advanced Technology in the Humanities, is transferring to digital form many of William Blake's illuminated books, paintings, drawings, and commercial illustrations. Central to the project will be scanned images of approximately 55 key copies of Blake's 19 illuminated books, about half of which will be reproduced for the first time. (For more information, WWW: http://jefferson.village.virginia.edu/blake/blake.wip-1.html). Bruce Graver, Providence College, Rhode Island, and Ronald Tetreault, Dalhousie University, are currently planning an electronic edition of Wordsworth, building on the wealth of material in the massive Cornell edition, but providing it in a more congenial hypertextual format (e-mail: beg@providence.edu).
3. See, for example, Peter L. Shillingsburg, 'An Inquiry into the Social Status of Texts and Modes of Textual Criticism', *Studies in Bibliography*, 42 (1989), 55-79.
4. 'The Complete Writings and Pictures of Dante Gabriel Rossetti: A Hypermedia Research Archive'. I am quoting from a description of the Rossetti project sent to me by Jerome McGann.
5. Jacques Derrida, 'Living On. Border Lines', in Harold Bloom, Paul de Man, Jacques Derrida, Geoffrey Hartman, and J. Hillis Miller, *Deconstruction and Criticism* (London and Henley: Routledge and Kegan Paul, 1979), 84.
6. G. Thomas Tanselle, 'Textual Criticism and Deconstruction', *Studies in Bibliography*, 43 (1990), 1-33; Jerome J. McGann, *The Textual Condition* (Princeton, N. J.: Princeton University Press, 1991), passim.
7. See, for example, G. P. Landow and P. Delany, eds., *Hypermedia and Literary Studies* (Cambridge, Mass.: MIT, 1991), 29-30.
8. Walter J. Ong, *Orality and Literacy: The Technologizing of the Word* (London: Methuen, 1982), 136-7.
9. A quotation from the Rossetti project description.
10. William Paulson, 'Computers, Minds, and Texts: Preliminary Reflections', *New Literary History*, 20 (1989), 291-303.
11. Thomas Carlyle, 'The Hero as Man of Letters', from *On Heroes, Hero-Worship, and the Heroic in History* (1841), extracted in Selected Writings, ed. Alan Shelston (Harmondsworth: Penguin, 1971), 233.
12. Ibid. 235.
13. S. T. Coleridrge, *Biographia Literaria* (2 vols, London, 1817), 1, 49-50.

We Are Already Beyond the Book[1]

George P. Landow
Department of English
Brown University

Predicting how we might move beyond the book requires, first, that we recognize ways we already find ourselves there. Most readers of a phrase like 'beyond the book' might assume that since books define much that seems most precious about our intellectual culture, such 'beyondness' could refer only to some fearful state that lay far ahead in the future. Glancing before ourselves now, however, reveals not an impossibly distant prospect but one waiting for us—as *Max Headroom,* the science-fiction TV series, puts it—'twenty minutes into the future'.

Until recently such a possibility meant exclusively moving into the analogue world of television and video and not, as it has increasingly happened, into the world of digital words and images—into, that is, an information technology comprising computerized text, images, sound, and video stored and read on geographically dispersed computers joined to form networks. In many ways, we have, for better or worse, already moved beyond the book. Even on the crudest, most materialist standard involving financial returns, we no longer find the book at the centre of our culture as the primary means of recording and disseminating information and entertainment. The sales of books and other printed matter, for centuries the centre of our technology of cultural memory, have now fallen to fourth position behind the sales of television, cinema, and video games. The video game, that child of the digital world, only recently displaced the book in third place on this list.

Since I have raised the crude, materialist factor of economics, let me point out another material instance of the way we find ourselves already beyond the book. As I have pointed out elsewhere, when many people first encounter the notion of electronic textuality and electronic books, they point out that reading on a computer screen—itself a transitory means of reading e-text—lacks many of the pleasures offered by the printed book.[2] Certainly, no one who has experienced the comparatively coarse resolution offered by most computer monitors would disagree with the obvious shortcomings of present-day computer technology, but many people who make this point do not stop here but proceed in such a way to make clear that their standard of comparison is not the books they actually encounter but rather some ideal utopian book, which in practice they never read and most contemporary students have never even handled.

A characteristic example of such illusions about present relation to the printed book presented itself at 'Beyond Gutenberg', a conference held at Yale University in the Spring of 1994. There Edward Tufte, the famous graphic and information designer, reminded his audience how many sensual pleasures books offer that computers do not. To make his point, he lovingly displayed Ben Jonson's own copy of Euclid, and his remarks made quite clear the way he presented this leather-bound volume from his own collection as the standard against which reading on computer screens should be judged. Upon the briefest consideration, using this exquisite, association-laden object to represent our experience of books appears intensely problematic. First, as everyone in the audience immediately recognized, this book, unlike most we use, is a unique object, an object quite unlike almost all we encounter in our daily experience of reading.

Taking the experience of American undergraduates today, a group of readers who read surrounded by analogue and digital information technologies of radio, cinema, television, video, and computing, we have to ask, 'What kind of books do they experience?' The answer has to be not the kind of books I did when, more than three decades ago, I was an undergraduate. Going to my college bookstore, I encountered hardcover anthologies, paperbound books, and inexpensive hardbound editions, such as those issued by Modern Library, Everyman, and the Oxford Classics. Today students still encounter comparatively expensive hardcover textbooks and anthologies, to be sure, and many of these, particularly in the physical and biological sciences, seem better illustrated and designed than those of my day. Many of the texts I assign, however, are paperbounds characterized by narrow margins, typographical errors, and tiny type. Anyone who has used such paperbacks can testify to the fact that many of them begin to collapse, break apart, and drop pages during the week in which they are assigned. In ascertaining the present and future position of the book in our culture, one must recognize the way most students today actually encounter the printed book as object. For them it offers not the sensual pleasures of the well-designed, well-printed, well-bound morocco volume of our ideal. Even more important, rather than embodying the relative permanence and sheer solidity so apparent in Jonson's Euclid (or, not to reach as high for an example, in clothbound Knopf editions of Wallace Stevens), books embody ill-designed, fragile, short-lived objects.

A good proportion of undergraduate reading in America, moreover, does not involve books at all. Since the invention of xerography, instructors by necessity have increasingly cobbled together their own anthologies of reading materials, often driven by the fact that long-used texts and anthologies have gone out of print. Ironically, at the very time that computer-based design tools have placed elegant book design within reach of the smallest publishers and book producers, the rise of these non-books offers ugly, undesigned, heterogeneous assemblages as a model for the reading-object. These cobbled-together non-books assemble collections of texts in different typefaces, design, reference conventions, and even page orientation. Such on-demand compilations play an increasingly important role in the reading experiences of many young adults today, and to them the book has lost both most of its aesthetic stature and its sense of solidity and permanence. Many of our students, in other words, have already found themselves somewhere beyond the book as solacing object and cultural paradigm. Which is not to say that they have moved beyond it to something better, to something that in any way surpasses Tufte's leather-bound volume. Instead, they have lost much of the experience of the book as we recall—and occasionally idealize—it.

We have also moved beyond the book in yet another way, for if by book we mean an object composed of printed pages of alphanumeric text between hard or soft covers, then a good deal of works until recently found only in this codex form have indeed moved 'beyond' this form. Difficult as it is for those of us who professionally work with books, whether as student, teacher, researcher, or writer, a great many—perhaps most—books do not contain literature, the arts, history, or even the sciences and social sciences. An enormous number of codex publications take the form of railroad and other schedules, regulations, parts and price lists, repair manuals, and the like. Even library catalogues, which in the Bodleian and British Library, still take the form of books, in most libraries long ago metamorphosed into file drawers of written and printed cards, and have now increasingly moved into the digital world. All the strengths of electronic text, including adaptability, infinite duplicability, and speed of transport, make these changes ultimately a means of saving time, energy, and other resources, particularly paper.

What implications does such a shift from physical to digital have for the culture of the book? Will it essentially leave unchanged the way readers consider novels, poetry, and non-fiction? Or will the fact that such works no longer always, or most conveniently, exist in book form in some way make the book as a form, as a means of reading and as a destination for writing, seem a trifle archaic, a bit, well, self-consciously 'high' culture? Each form of physically recording a text has its peculiar strengths and weaknesses, to be sure. What, then, are those associated with the new digital technologies of cultural memory?

An indication of some of these costs and benefits appears if we consider Tufte's warnings about the shortcomings of digitization. From his point of view one of the chief problems in computing lies in the coarse resolution available on contemporary computer screens. Holding up an exquisitely printed map from the eighteenth or nineteenth century, he claimed that such printed sources of information have a resolution thousands of times finer than that available on standard monitors. Tufte is correct: at present inadequate screen technology means that information on computer monitors cannot come close to providing the resolution or aesthetic pleasure provided by such (albeit rare) printed documents.

Of course, this matter of resolution is not the entire story, and against Tufte's fine-grained map I would like to juxtapose an example of an electronic one that more than makes up for its comparatively poor resolution by offering interactivity, adaptability, and ease of obtaining the information required by individual users. My example comes from the Berlin U-bahn or subway system, which now offers travellers a touch-screen guide that exemplifies the strengths of computerized information. The traveller in need of information encounters a first screen with images of different kinds of public transportation and directions in three languages. Touching the first screen produces another that permits one to choose Dutch, English, French, German, Polish, Spanish, or Turkish versions. At this point one can request information about U-bahn stations, stations plus bus stops, street addresses, or special destinations. Choosing 'Special Destinations', one receives a choice of embassies and consulates, museums, places of interest, theatres, concerts and events, hotels, universities, hospitals, and so on. Touching 'Museums' produces a screen divided alphabetically; choosing B produces a list of which the first six entries are: Bauhaus Archiv, Berlin-Museum, Berliner Hand-werkersmuseum, Berliner Kinomuseum, Berlinische Galerie, and Bodemuseum. Pressing the name of the intended destination brings up a series of screens that permit one to indicate the date and time of day one wishes to travel. At this point one receives a simple diagram indicating the station from which to depart, any necessary changes, and the scheduled times of arrival and departure of all trains involved. If dissatisfied with the resulting plan, one can request alternate routes; if satisfied, one prints out one's route and schedule. It is also possible to use the U-bahn kiosk to plan one's travel to individual street addresses.

As this example shows, a computerized information source, which forms the digital analogue to a set of street maps, subway and bus schedules, and so forth, offers ample gains to make up for its obvious losses. Although attractively designed, it does not have, and does not need, the printed map's fine-grained detail, which it trades for vastly greater ease of use and increased information. The comparison of the printed map to the digital travel planner reminds us of several key matters, the first of which is that translating such information resources into computerized form produces something quite new. The digital resource boasts speed, ease of use, and adaptability, and where these are crucial factors, they will allow it to displace the printed reference. Returning to Tufte's comparison, one also realizes that fine-grained detail does not always equate either to more information or to more easily usable information.

For the reasons displayed by the Berlin U-bahn kiosk, electronic text seems certain to displace certain kinds of printed matter, even that in books, though not, to be sure, those upon which most in the academic world have directed their attention. Nonetheless, we must recognize the changes that take place, both because they remind us more fully what is included in the notions of 'book' (and moving 'beyond' it) and because they suggest the extent to which people will increasingly turn to non-book-like objects for their textual information.

Printed Books Are Technology, Too

As these last remarks indicate, we have already moved far enough beyond the book that we find ourselves, for the first time in centuries, able to see the book as unnatural, as a near-miraculous technological innovation and not as something intrinsically and inevitably human. We can, to use Derridean terms, de-centre the book. We find ourselves in the position, in other words, of perceiving the book *as technology*. I think it no mere coincidence that it is at precisely this period in human history we have acquired crucial intellectual distance from the book as object and as cultural product. First came the distant hearing—the telephone—then the cinema and then the distant seeing of television. It is only with the added possibilities created by these new information media and computing that Harold Innis, Marshall McLuhan, Jack Goody, Elizabeth Eisenstein, Alvin Kernan, Roger Chartier, and the European scholars of *Lesengeshichte* could arise.

Influential as these scholars have been, not all scholars willingly recognize the power of information technologies upon culture. This resistance appears in two characteristic reactions to the proposition that information technology constitutes a crucial cultural force. First, one encounters a tendency among many humanists contemplating the possibility that information technology influences culture to assume that before now, before computing, our intellectual culture existed in some pastoral non-technological realm. *Technology*, in the lexicon of many humanists, generally means 'only that technology of which I am frightened'. In fact, I have frequently heard humanists use the word technology to mean 'some intrusive, alien force like computing' as if pencils, paper, typewriters, and printing presses were in some way *natural*. Digital technology may be new, but technology, particularly information technology, has permeated all known culture since the beginnings of human history. If we hope to discern the ways in which we might move beyond the book, we must not treat all previous information technologies of language, rhetoric, writing, and printing as non-technological.

A second form of resistance to recognizing the role of information technology in culture appears in implicit claims that technology, particularly information technology, can *never* have cultural effects. Almost always presented by speakers and writers as evidence of their own sophistication and sensitivity, this strategy of denial has an unintended effect: denying that Gutenberg's invention or television can exist in a causal connection to any other aspect of culture immediately transforms technology—whatever the author means by that term—into a kind of intellectual monster, something so taboo that civilized people cannot discuss it in public. In other words, it takes technology, which is both an agent and effect of our continually changing culture(s), and denies its existence as an element of human culture. One result appears in the strategies of historical or predictive studies that relate cultural phenomena to all sorts of economic, cultural, and ideological factors but avert their eyes from any technological causation, as if it, and only it, were in some way reductive. The effect, of course, finally is to deny that this particular form of cultural product can have any effect.

We have to remind ourselves that if, how, and whenever we move beyond the book, that movement will not embody a movement from something natural or human to something artificial—from nature to technology—since writing, and printing, and books are about as technological as one can be. Books, after all, are teaching and communicating *machines*.

From Physical Mark to Code

These new digital information technologies involve fundamental changes in the way we read and write, and these radical differences in turn derive from a single fact, the shift from the physical to the virtual. As I have explained elsewhere,

> Text-based computing provides us with electronic rather than physical texts, and this shift from ink to electronic code—what Jean Baudrillard calls the shift from the 'tactile' to the 'digital'—produces an information technology that simultaneously combines fixity and flexibility, order and accessibility—but at a cost. Since electronic text-processing is a matter of manipulating computer-manipulated codes, all texts that the writer encounters on the screen are virtual texts. Using an analogy to optics, computer scientists speak of 'virtual machines' created by an operating system that provides individual users with the experience of working on their own individual machines when they in fact share a system with as many as several hundred others. Similarly, all texts the reader and the writer encounter on a computer screen exist as a version created specifically for them while an electronic primary version resides in the computer's memory. One therefore works on an electronic copy until such time as both versions converge when the writer commands the computer to 'save' her version of the text by placing it in memory. At this point the text on screen and in the computer's memory briefly coincide, but the reader always encounters a virtual image of the stored text and not the original version itself; in fact, when one describes electronic wordprocessing, such terms and such distinctions no longer make much sense.[3]

All such moving beyond the book derives directly from a single defining characteristic of the digital word. Unlike all previous forms of textuality, the digital word is virtual, not physical. Earlier kinds of text required physical marks on physical surfaces. The image, sign, letter, or number was scratched into a physical surface, such as stone or clay, or written upon a surface with some sort of pigment. These marks, which so obviously created a visible physical record of invisible sounds, provided a technology of cultural memory that, as Plato and many others since have pointed out, has had defining effects on human culture. However fragile the written record, it nonetheless marks a wonderful freezing of something otherwise evanescent, and from the time of the ancient Egyptians authors have often believed that written records of speech conferred a kind of permanence and immortality upon the writer of those words.

Many other technological inventions mark the history of information technology, from the development of writing to that of the printing press. These include the inventions of the alphabet, scrolls, the codex, and inexpensive writing surfaces. Printing, the appearance of which marks a great dividing line in human history, represents the next great landmark in information technology. Printing adds two major qualities to the written, physically existing text—multiplicity and fixity—that have enormous consequences for the way we conceive of ourselves and our culture. The printing press creates large numbers of copies of essentially the same text. As McLuhan, Eisenstein, and others have argued, the effects of this range across fundamental conceptions about education, scholarship, intellectual property, and the self. To take a simple example: the availability of many copies of the same text not only, as Benjamin realized, removed the aura of the unique object, it also fundamentally changed the way people think about preserving information. The keeper of manuscripts tries to slow their inevitable degradation (which is caused by the act of reading them) and the errors introduced by copyists. The person who would preserve information in a manuscript age does so by preventing readers from having access to the text, since such readers inevitably lead to its destruction. In an age of printing the person who would preserve a text does so, in contrast, by disseminating it as widely as possible.

Each form of physically recording a text has its peculiar qualities, qualities that often have far greater cultural effect than might at first appear. Even something as apparently trivial as the availability of relatively inexpensive writing materials can have unexpected, and unexpectedly great, effects. The great cost of writing surfaces led scribes to cram in as many letters as possible, so that written text omitted spaces between words. This economic factor made reading an act of decipherment, a craft skill generally available only to a few. The introduction of inexpensive writing surfaces led, around the year 1000, to interword spacing, and that crucial invention permitted reading silently, which, in turn, led to our modern notions of a private, interior self.

What are the crucial, defining qualities, then, of the new digital technologies of cultural memory? One, above all, stands out: whereas all previous forms of writing involve physical marks on a physical surface, in digital information technology writing takes the form of a series of codes. The resulting textuality is virtual, fluid, adaptable, open, capable of being processed, capable of being infinitely duplicated, capable of being moved about rapidly, capable, finally, of being net-work-able—of being joined with other texts.

All fundamental characteristics of the world of digital information derive directly from this shift of modes—a shift made apparent, one realizes, by the fact that one never reads the text 'itself', since that record resides invisibly in the computer's memory. Instead, one reads a virtual version of that text on a screen or other display device. By removing the text one step from its physical instantiation, a number of changes occur, the most obvious of which is that the difference between the text and the object on which it appears becomes starkly clear. As literary theorists have emphasized for decades, one must distinguish between the text itself and its physical embodiment in a particular delivery vehicle, reading site, or machine. Digital information technology permits us to perceive that books, printed books, are machines just as are computers that handle or present text.

Once textuality abandons the simply physical form of earlier writing, it also abandons some of its relations to economy and scale. For example, one can reproduce a digitally stored text an indefinite number of times without in any way affecting it, lessening it, wearing away at it. Duplicating a manuscript requires that one expend an amount of time and energy similar to that expended in the creation of the text one wishes to copy. Duplicating a text by printing it with metal type or cast plates offers far greater economies of scale, but eventually the metal begins to wear—a fact readily apparent to students of engraved images. Duplicating a text stored electronically, however, has no such effect and therefore permits—and even encourages—an enormously larger number of copies.

Digital textuality also permits far greater ease of manipulatibilty and reconfigurabilty. As anyone who has used a wordprocessor quickly perceives, one can easily search through a text or reconfigure its appearance.[4] One result of recording text in the form of electronic codes, rather than in that of physical marks, permits the creation of so-called markup languages that permit the appearance of entire texts to be reconfigured rapidly. Recording a text by handwriting, typewriter, or typesetting device involves performative—as opposed to descriptive—markup. In other words, when one begins a new paragraph while writing with a typewriter (or a computer used inappropriately as one), one either skips a line, or indents a specific number of spaces, or employs some other convention. When using a so-called mark-up language (or *markup* for short), one simply marks the beginning and ending of that unit of text with standard symbols, such as <p> and </p>, which permit readers and writers (depending on the system) to reconfigure the appearance of paragraphs.

Such an approach to textuality allows the economical reuse of texts, since one can automatically reconfigure the same text, say, for a personal printer, typesetting device, or electronic display simply by redefining the value of each symbol. Such markup, for example, also permits readers to reconfigure the appearance of a scholarly text, so that one could toggle back and forth between a modern annotated edition of a eighteenth-century text and its original appearance upon its publication, including typeface, font size, and colour of paper.

Connecting computers together in networks adds another series of qualities to digital textuality. Digitizing text permits one to reproduce, manipulate, and reconfigure it with great ease and rapidity. Connecting computers together in the form of digital networks enables one to move such text from one storage and reading site to another. Until the world of networked digital information technology, disseminating a text required physically moving it from one place to another. Non-networked digital technology still has the same limitations, and today an enormous amount of digital information is still stored and moved on tapes, floppy disks, Syquest cartridges, CD-ROMs, and so on. But as electronic bulletin boards, discussion lists, and the World Wide Web make clear, many readers and writers have already moved beyond the book into such essentially location-independent texts and textbases.[5]

Notes

1. This essay has been taken from the first section of my 'Twenty Minutes into the Future, or How Are We Moving beyond the Book?,' *The Future of the Book*, ed. Geoffrey Nunberg, which the University of California Press and Brepols will publish later in 1996. This volume includes the papers delivered at the August 1994 conference of the same name that Geoffrey Nunberg and Umberto Eco organized in San Marino (Italy). I would like to thank Dr. Nunberg for granting permission to use my essay in this volume.
2. "What's a Critic to Do? Critical Theory in the Age of Hypertext," in *Hyper/Text/Theory*, ed. Landow (Baltimore: Johns Hopkins University Press, 1994), 3-6.
3. *Hypertext: The Convergence of Contemporary Critical Theory and Technology* (Baltimore: Johns Hopkins University Press, 1992), xx. For Jean Baudrillard, see *Simulations*, trans. Paul Foss, Paul Patton, and Philip Beitchman (New York: Semiotext(e), 1983), 115.
4. Michael Heim's *Electric Language: A Philosophical Study of Word Processing* (New Haven: Yale University Press, 1987) and Richard Lanham's *Electronic Word: Democracy, Technology, and The Arts* (Chicago: University of Chicago Press, 1993) both eloquently describe the nature and implications of wordprocessing.

5. For the notion of location-independent textbases, see Christinger Tomer, "Emerging Electronic Library Services and the Idea of Location Independence" in Landow and Delany, *The Digital Word: Text-Based Computing in the Humanities* (Cambridge, Mass.: MIT Press, 1993), 139-62.

Connectionism and the Posthumanities

Sadie Plant
Department of Philosophy
University of Warwick

Like all studies of culture, those which prioritize the impact of new technologies tend to be conducted from a humanist perspective which is itself called into question by the processings and telecommunications of the computer age. Digitization is re-engineering the media, economies, the arts and the sciences with a complete lack of discretion or regard for the differences in kind which once kept them apart. The population of computers and connections between them is growing exponentially, as are the areas in which they operate. Self-organizing processes begin to emerge, not only in assemblages which can easily be defined as machines, but also amongst and between markets, eco-systems, micro-biotic activities and, of course, in the neuro-chemical processes of human consciousness. None of these complex assemblages are discrete, unified, or guided by some form of central strategy. Complex systems need neither external nor internal government: they are neither controlled nor self-controlled. They are neither seeking after some pre-ordained point nor following a route dictated by their past, but instead they are engineering themselves from the bottom up. And since they are processes rather than things, complex assemblages can only be named for a moment which will always miss them happening. This is the problem for any theoretical position which considers itself to be coming from some place immune from their effects. Which is more or less to say: this is the problem for theory itself as well, of course, as for those who theorize.

Modern conceptions of theory are inevitably developed from the position of exteriority assumed by an anthropocentric world view; entangled with the humanist ideals of progress, reason, and agency; and inseparable from the disciplines and institutions in which they are inscribed. In this respect, all the faculties are humanities: the arts and sciences alike are grounded in some conception of historical purpose and human destiny. As for the academy which exercises these disciplines: man is the centre of its world and the point of its investigations.

It is this emphasis on agency which has ensured that theories of culture tend towards representations of technology, rather than its material effects. Theories and histories of machinery, media, communications, and other technical developments are really concerned with humans, not machines; their interests lie with the question of what the technology means for man and the course of his history. With the exception of Marshall McLuhan's work, television, for example, has tended to be studied in terms of the content and reception of its images rather than its functioning as a telecommunications system. Along with all other aspects of computing culture, the Net now meets with the same response. Interest is expressed in its users, their messages, their lifestyles, intentions, and perspectives, but as an interconnected system emergent from its own connections, it is largely unexplored. Human interest is overriding, with the consequence that even the most complex machines are still referred to as tools, or toys: things with which man can work on a nature and play in a reality for which he holds himself responsible.

If it is to have any purchase on the tendencies and syndromes it analyses, theory must lose these anthropocentric associations. Not in favour of some random sense in which anything goes, but in order to become compatible with the processes theory once described, behaving as they behave, and so engineering, extending, and replicating itself. Theory must stop being theoretical in the moment it begins to connect with the software engineerings it has to become. It too becomes a matter of simulation and replication, adding to the complexities it might once have been content to represent.

Connectionism is hunting some way of connecting the complex systems which arise in what were once distinct and relatively closed orders of disciplined knowledge. Insofar as connectionism is a theory (which is not very far at all), it suggests that what modernity conceives as states, structures, and organisms are reductionist representations of dynamic processes functioning at molecular levels and much larger scales. As it interacts with the study of culture, it discovers these patterns within and beyond orthodox conceptions of both the individual and the collective, and reconfigures subjects and societies as complexities of connections, communications, and communicating systems.

Connectionism is a term which has emerged from a variety of once disparate areas: chemistry, biology, psychology, and researches in Artificial Intelligence. It is used to define the processes which occur in and between systems which lack any central principle or hierarchical structure, but instead evolve by 'pulling themselves up by their own bootstraps', according to their own immanent rules of organization. In the wake of the computer revolution and, in particular, the possibilities of miniaturization and mathematical simulation it unfolds, these processes can be tracked in chemical clocks, evolutionary programs, neural nets, and ecological systems. Such assemblages are defined as complex because they defy definition from any point external to themselves; because they have only the most contingent and temporary boundaries; because they maintain themselves by reference to their own internal composition; and also because they are characterized by unpredictable growth and development. Complex systems do not evolve with the regularities and linearities previously ascribed to living or functioning systems, but are instead marked by the leaps and bounds of bifurcatory moments in which everything—including behavioural rules—is subject to sudden and wholesale change. To human eyes, the change from ice to water may appear to happen smoothly, continuously, on a single scale, and because of external intervention—i.e. the application of heat—but it is really (or also) an effect of microscopic and simultaneous communications occurring between the ice molecules which effectively 'make a decision' to melt at precisely the same time.

Connectionism describes the processes of interlinking by which such systems change and grow. Its emergence in the sciences is already rewriting some of the most basic modern conceptions of evolutionary programming, geological activity, chemical processing and organic life. Its implications for the study of human culture are equally devastating to modern presuppositions about the special status and privileged role of the human species, and equally full of promise for the development of an approach to individual, socio-economic, and geo-political cultural life which might facilitate new and pertinent approaches to those complex systems which persist in these zones. Brains, cities, banking systems, traffic problems, literary texts, epidemiological patterns, and so-called 'sub-cultures' are exemplary cases of assemblages open to a connectionist approach.

Although they are amongst the last of the faculties to find a place in the academic system, the humanities name the overriding impetus which governs education and research and, by extension, the disciplining of all knowledge. It is to further, reproduce, and pass on the ROM of something understood as human history: the modern project *par excellence.*

As humanism emerges from the ruins of theism, it does not remove some notion of centralized agency, but merely multiplies it. Where once there was God, now there is man, centred, integrated, autonomous, and with a past he can call his own, a history whose progress he is destined to reproduce, and establishing education as an essentially humanizing process invested in the 'dignity of man'.

Alan Bullock, author of the 1970s Bullock Reports, gives an eloquent account of the humanist conception of education. It is, he writes:

> designed not as a training in specific tasks or techniques, but as an awakening to the possibilities of human life, a drawing out or cultivation of a young man's or a young woman's human-ness. Some people are born with this awareness and their potentialities unfold naturally. But for the majority it needs to be evoked. Hence not only the central importance humanists have always attributed to education but also the broad terms in which they have conceived it as grounded in a general education, aimed at the all-round development of the personality and of the full range of an individuals' talents.[1]

The details of its newly discovered history of humanity will be shared only with those who are willing and able to nurture and protect it: those who are successfully humanized. The modern education system guarantees that intelligence is monopolized by the educated, which is to say that they have been successfully turned into good humans, well behaved and responsible members of the species who will do nothing but reproduce both the knowledges and the institutions in which they are taught.

It is this quest to safeguard or evoke what Bullock calls 'human-ness' which underwrites the modern education system and, by extension, all the disciplines of modernity. It may sound harmless enough, but as Foucault's work makes abundantly clear, the organization of knowledge and the disciplining of intelligence is crucial to the functioning of power itself. In the secondary sector, where a centrally organized curriculum is taught between bells, tests, detentions, and assemblies, not to mention the horrors of compulsory physical education, it is easy to see the extent to which the education system disciplines as it teaches. Schools are deeply entangled with the orders of the asylum, the prison, the hospital and, by extension, the army and the factory, and educational practice is continuous with the political authorities and moral codes which have their most brutal impact on all they define as mad, bad, sick, or perverted. The regulations of undergraduate and graduate life may be less overtly displayed, but the universities make it equally clear that education is a matter of social control. As Foucault writes, 'the university stands for the institutional apparatus through which society ensures its uneventful reproduction, at the least cost to itself.'[2] Not only are students policed, examined, and classified, but the mission statements of higher educational institutions commit them to both the furthering of excellence in higher learning, and also the inculcation of the values necessary to the production of good citizens.

There is of course a whole history of challenges to education, the academy, and the role of its intellectuals, disciplines, and students. In the mid-1960s, a new area called Cultural Studies began to intervene on all these fronts. Pioneering interdisciplinary research, it promoted student-based learning, showed an unprecedented interest in what had hitherto been known as 'low culture', and reconfigured traditional conceptions of the intellectual and the role of theory itself.

Its emergence was concurrent with many other such contestations of the old system: throughout the 1960s, and across the West, radicalized students and intellectuals were experimenting with new non-hierarchical and cross-disciplinary modes of teaching and research. *On the Poverty of Student Life*, a notorious pamphlet which circulated in Paris the year before the 'May events', made a stark and pertinent attack on a system devoted only to the reproduction of the socio-economic and political status quo, and occupying students demanded to write their own curricula and mark their own exams. The events of 1968 were clearly, and amongst many other things, the beginnings of an unprecedented challenge to modernity's knowledges and politics. As Foucault writes, 'the individuals who were subjected to the educational system, to the most constraining forms of conservatism and repetition, fought a revolutionary battle' and 'effectively ended the form of higher education that began in the nineteenth century— the curious set of institutions that transformed a small proportion of the young into a social elite.' But this still 'leaves the full range of hidden mechanisms through which a society conveys its knowledge and ensures its survival under the mask of knowledge: newspapers, television, technical schools, and the lycee (even more than the university).'3

Immanuel Wallerstein argues that it was the failure of 1968 that led disillusioned intellectuals to 'see "culture" as an alternative arena in which at last human action might be efficacious'.5 But if 1968 was indeed a crucial break, cultural studies began its climb out of the disciplines some years before the barricades went up. And with it came a good deal of intellectual baggage from the days before the events, much of which allowed it to develop not as a discipline, but a project or, more precisely, 'the' project: a unified political direction entirely invested in the destiny of man. What Wallerstein calls 'human action' becomes the literal be all and end all of cultural studies. Its interdisciplinarity was confined to those elements from the arts and social sciences which could be enlisted in the service of a peculiarly modern, and already disciplined, notion of human agency.6

Ironically, both its political and academic histories have conspired to turn Cultural Studies away from such an approach and into the exemplary case of that most modern of disciplinary zones, the one that epitomizes and legitimizes the intellectual status, themes, and methodologies of the sciences and the arts, and the one which underwrites modern conceptions of education itself: the humanities.

Cultural Studies absorbed Foucault, but had no interest in his reports from the dark side of its disciplines, preferring instead to see his work as a variant on its own humanist discourse and remaining untouched by the inhuman and undisciplined zones his writing traversed. If Cultural Studies was ever subversive, it did not intend things to go this far: its political project was never to destroy the social order, but merely to humanize it. The end of authorship became another framework, Foucault's complex genealogies were confined to matters of textual interest, and the discipline of Cultural Studies was safe.

If the modern academy has survived both the political onslaughts of the 1960s and the antihumanism of Foucault, it is not so easy for it to deal with an increasingly computed culture. The academy loses its control over intelligence once it is even possible to imagine a situation in which information can be accessed from nets which care for neither old boy status nor exam results. There is no selection on the Net. Beyond the ability to buy, beg, borrow, or steal, there are no requirements to be fulfilled before a CD-ROM can be used. But even these are the more superficial effects of a deep rewiring of the processes by which knowledge is disciplined and reproduced.

As the role of the human teacher of machines is subsumed by their ability to learn for themselves, the science of artificial intelligence mutates into the engineering of artificial life. The top-down imposition of knowledge becomes redundant, and anything which might be called growth, evolution, or development occurs in systems which function without such external governors or even centralized controls of their own. They have no pre-ordained designs or goals in sight, but proceed bottom-up, making connections and reinforcing links, in precisely the way that synapses function in the human brain with which they converge as neural nets.

These connections between the parallel distributed processings of machines, brains, and an immense complexity of other dynamic communications systems have enormous implications for all conceptions of teaching, learning, and the disciplining of knowledge. Released from its relation to teaching, learning is no longer coded as study and confined to some particular zone, specialized behaviour, or compartmentalized period of time. The teacher no longer controls the process, ensuring the development of well-rounded individuals one step at a time, serial fashion, but, if anything, simply gives students --- or software systems—the wherewithal to explore for themselves. The digitization of what might be called the world's virtual library of knowledge reconfigures volumes and disciplinary zones into the passages and abstracts of hypertext systems which function regardless of canons and set texts. Collapsing disciplinary boundaries and distinctions between the producers and consumers of information, Bush's protohypertext, the memex, and Nelson's Xanadu undo Read Only Memory once and for all.

Not that much of this has yet hit home. While technical and economic imperatives have forced some moves from teaching to learning in the universities, higher education remains premised on the paternal function of the professorial figure, handing his knowledge down through the generations, restricting access, and preserving a tradition still in debt to the Greeks. As Foucault writes, 'humanism is based on the desire to change the ideological system without altering institutions; and reformers wish to change the institution without touching the ideological system.'[7] The trick is to make them both happen at once. And more than this, 'it isn't enough to suppress or overturn the university. Other forms of repression must also be attacked.'[8]

If intelligence can neither be taught nor confined to a few humans, it cannot even be monopolized by all of them: machines learn, and learning is a machinic process, a matter of communication, connection, and material self-organization.

The emergence of machine intelligence coincides with the discovery that machines are complex systems, and complex systems are everywhere, from the microbiological to the macroeconomic, and across what were once distinct natural, social, human, and artificial zones. These are assemblages 'at the edge of order and chaos' whose components 'never quite lock into place, yet never quite dissolve into turbulence, either. These are the systems that are both stable enough to store information, and yet evanescent enough to transmit it. These are the systems that can be organized to perform complex computations, to react to the world, to be spontaneous, adaptive, and alive.'9

By a suitably piecemeal, discontinuous process marked by simultaneous emergences and lateral connections, connectionism begins to make the move from the representation to the fabrication of culture. While both theory and high culture have been challenged by Cultural Studies, it has done little to make either of them disappear, not least because, in spite of its best intentions and because of the demarcations of knowledge with which it has had to work, it has continued to be conducted both 'in theory' and way up in the ivory towers. Its critiques, no matter how pertinent, have had little material effect on the cultures with which they engage, and its attention to mass, low, sub, and popular cultures has allowed few of its studies to become as popular as the cultures with which they engage.

A connectionist approach necessitates and facilitates new ways of writing culture which no longer stand above and comment on something considered their subject or object of research, but instead become components of the material processes they write about. Hence Deleuze and Guattari's comment that there should be no difference between a book and what it writes about, and their claim to be doing pop analysis. This has less to do with the extent to which their books are read and their thoughts directly consumed than with continuities between what is written and what happens elsewhere. Trance dancers don't need Deleuze and Guattari to teach them about bodies without organs and rhizomatic connections: they have learned all this for themselves. No longer a question of describing or interpreting events taking place in the culture elsewhere, writing becomes a process of software engineering, a matter of producing intensities, making connections, and connecting with the other connectionist systems and their connections too. Deleuze writes of a theory that 'does not totalize', but 'is an instrument for multiplication and it also multiplies itself.'10

This is not a question of applying theory, nor even of integrating theory and practice in some new dialectical relation, but something more akin to what Deleuze refers to as a 'system of relays within a larger sphere, within a multiplicity of parts that are both theoretical and practical.' The theorist is never alone: 'Who speaks and acts? It is always a multiplicity, even within the person who speaks and acts. All of us are 'groupuscules'. Representation no longer exists; there's only action - theoretical action and practical action which serve as relays and form networks.'11

Humans are no longer the sole agents of intelligence. This is why connectionism is so closely allied to what can only be called the posthumanities. The humanities' subjects, the human subjects, and the educational institutions which have devoted themselves to their reproduction are equally undermined. The collapse of the modern disciplines not only opens onto a new interdisciplinary space, but also takes the ground from under the feet of the integrated, unified individual. Complex bio-chemical processes function within, across, and in between what were once conceived as autonomous agents, corroding the boundaries between man, nature, and the tools with which he has mediated this relationship. The histories written as the histories of humanity can no longer maintain their independence from emergent processes in the economies and complex systems with which they interact, and attempts to define culture in the ideological, humanist, and socio-political terms which have provided its post-war framework merely perpetuate a distinction between the human, the machinic, and the so-called natural which underwrites modernity's techniques of policing knowledge and reality.

Beyond spectacular society and speculative humanism there is an emergent complexity, an evolving intelligence in which all material life is involved: all thinking, writing, dancing, engineering, creativity, social organization, biological processing, economic interaction, and communication of every kind. It is the matrix, the virtuality, and the future of every separated thing, individuated organism, disciplined idea, and social structure. Its impact on the academy, its disciplines, and the humanism which guides the educational process is itself interconnected with a multiplicity of other effects in once distinct and separated zones. The telecoms revolution and the complex systems with which it coincides are not merely re-engineering the university, but the very conditions of modernity.

The posthuman cultures which emerge are complex systems; self-organizing assemblages in a perpetual motion of connection and exchange with a multiplicity of their own environments. They are marked by bifurcations and cross-currents, phase transitions and tendencies replicated across them all. They are fractal contexts, folding, enveloping, and twisting back on each other; irreducible to their states and uncontainable by their representations. They are not things to be studied, but paths to be traced and routes to be travelled by connectionist writings with no faith to keep, no central points or sources, and no reasons to conclude. Theories, studies, and narratives mutate into nomadic adventures and post-disciplinary explorations; unsolicited and often unwelcome experiments which proceed without ideological conceptions and evade all moral imperatives. The study of self-replicating processes and self-organizing systems is also, necessarily, their engineering.

Notes

1. Bullock, Alan, (1985) *The Humanist Tradition in the West* (New York and London: WW Norton, 1985), 156.
2. Michel Foucault, 'Revolutionary Action: Until Now', in Michel Foucault, *Language, Counter-memory, Practice*, ed. Donald Bouchard (New York: Cornell University Press, 1977), 224.
3. Ibid. 223.

4. Ibid. 225.

5. Immanuel Wallerstein, *Geopolitics and Geocultures, Essays on the changing world system,* (Cambridge, 1991), .

6. Ibid. 12.

7. Foucault (1977), .

8. Ibid. 224.

9. M. Mitchell Waldrop, *Complexity, The Emerging Science at the Edge of Order and Chaos* (London: Viking, 1992), 293.

10. Michel Foucault and Gilles Deleuze, 'Intellectuals and Power', in Michel Foucault, *Language, Counter-memory, Practice,* 208.

11. Ibid. 206.

Hypermedia: When Will They Feel Natural?

John Pickering
Psychology Department
Warwick University

Preamble: A Conversation

As the culture of the book mingles with the new culture of hypermedia, conversations like the one below can be overheard. Acolyte (A), a PhD student, is talking to two professors. One is Bookdon (B) who, while a kindly, authoritative figure, nonetheless clasps his copy of *The Uses of Literacy* with an air of defensive uncertainty. The other, business-like and briskly confident, is Cyberdon (C), who divides her attention between the conversation and her laptop computer. The latter, from time to time, emits a soft electronic clang to indicate the arrival of another communication from the Internet.

> A: I would like to know why Whitman called that poem *I Sing the Body Electric*. I mean, why *Electric*? What did he know of electricity in 1855?

> B: Hm, interesting. Not my area of course, but I think I'd start by by looking at a good biography and then perhaps try Killinsworth's *Whitman's Poetry of the Body*. You could also look at who was writing near his time on scientific things. Beaver's *The Science Fiction of Edgar Allen Poe* and Marx's *Machine in the Garden* could both be useful in a general sort of way. You might have a chat with old Tomefondle. I think he did something on machine images in poetry once, or was it ships? I forget ...

> C: Email Max Modem at San Diego, the address is *maxmod@ucsd.edu*. Got that? Ok. He may not do much on Whitman now, but he can bounce your message on to someone who does. He'll probably mail you back some grad course notes and stuff like that. In fact, I think he's got a hypertext web on his public access file that deals with American poetry of that era. It's neat, movies and all, comes up really well on Netscape. You could download that so long as you've got the right URL tools. I'd use Fetch, Mosaic is too slow. What sort of machine do you have?

> A: Well, at the moment I've only got an old PC, but there's a really good Quadra in the department that I can use. I hope to be getting a laptop of some sort and I might just be able to afford a CD-ROM

drive, but then I'd have to do with less RAM. It's hard to know the best options . . .

B: Excuse me . . .

C: Well, whatever you do, make sure it's got the 486DX4-100 processor and at least eight megabytes on board so you can have a really meaty cache memory. Anything else and you can't get on because the disk keeps on kicking in and out . . .

A: Yes, and when Janet clogs up, well, you might as well forget it.

C: Right, working online with the Internet can be a pain. If traffic gets too heavy I just logout and do something stand-alone. That reminds me, I've come across this really neat hypertext tool, Networx or something like that. It needs a reasonable platform mind you . . .

B: Er . . . excuse me . . . Whitman? How about looking through recent numbers of *American Literary Studies*? There's usually some good stuff in it, though where it's got to now they've moved the journals to make room for those wretched computer thingies I've no idea.

A: Oh, yes, well, first I think I'll do a search on the LITFAX database. Some keywords like 'Whitman', 'Body' and 'Electr-' with a wildcard. If there's too much I'll sort it by date and work back from the most recent entries. They're more likely to be downloadable in any case. How does that sound?

C: Sharp!

B: Incomprehensible. (This is said, softly and sadly, as he fades into the computer-free zone of his study).

While this vignette is a caricature, it is now a commonplace suggestion that hypermedia are the coming vehicle for literacy. It is proposed we are in a state of transition, where the torch of literary culture is being passed. The passing generation are those who feel most at ease with ink on paper, libraries, and marginalia, the homely low-tech culture of the book. But these amiable dinosaurs, it seems, are about to be engulfed by a new culture of electronic textuality with its jargon of hypermedia scholarship. The Internet, the World Wide Web, URL tools, and hypermedia all promote the rapid movement of texts and the interpretation of and responses to those texts. This, it appears, is to be the stuff of a new academic culture as, in the postmodern condition, it participates in a mobile and fluid play of signification that is part of what Baudrillard has called the 'ecstasy of communication'.[1]

This essay is a brief inquiry into some consequences of the new culture. After an introductory observation on cultural evolution, it will deal with the interaction between hypermedia and book culture and with some changes that this interaction may bring, particularly to what feels authoritative. One conclusion that will be drawn is that there are limits to these changes. These limits have to do with the nature of narrative.

On Evolution

The explosive growth of information technology over the past few decades is part of an acceleration of cultural evolution. While it is more usual to think of evolution as progressive biological change in plants and animals, human evolution is now more a matter of cultural change. Cultural evolution has to do with the progressive development of tools and practices and, more centrally to what is being dealt with here, with the interior trace that accompanies these technological developments and which modifies human consciousness. This trace may have deeper roots that even McLuhan suspected in saying: 'When technology extends our senses a new translation of culture occurs as swiftly as the new technology is interiorized.'[2]

In fact, recent developments in evolutionary theory suggest that as well as being genetically programmed, complex creatures like human beings are far more open to environmental shaping during their development than previously thought. Since human beings also modify the environment, adapting it to their needs by purposive action, the successive generations who develop within this adapted environment thereby receive both a genetic and a cultural inheritance. Human evolution, far from being the mere survival of accidents, is also, somewhat as Lamarck and Bergson surmised, a matter of self-creation through purposive action.[3]

Human adaptive modification of the environment occurs on a massive and problematic scale. Human beings develop within a cultural environment which is a human creation and from which they assimilate fundamental aspects of their psychological makeup. The human condition is thus self-produced within a reflexive semiotic system which encompasses cultural and biological levels of order and which blurs the boundary in the process. This system embraces tools as well as genes, skills as well as reflexes, and beliefs as well as instincts. The mind is not an absolute of nature, but a process supported by a system of mutually evolved relationships. Human mental life, with its skills and values, is not fixed or predetermined but is reformed again and again as the tools and practices of the cultural *milieu* are assimilated by successive generations. [4]

Now cultural evolution has accelerated to the point where biological change is, on the human timescale, practically irrelevant.[5] In very rough terms, the time between significant milestones in human cultural evolution is about a tenth of the previous one. Thus, while tool culture is known to be well over five hundred thousand years old, about fifty thousand years ago there was a marked jump in the sophistication and diversity of tools made, which may well have been associated with developments in cultural transmission. Writing appeared about five thousand years ago and, in the west at least, Gutenberg makes the textual foundations of common culture only about five hundred years old. The remarkable technological innovations of the last fifty years or so have transformed these foundations, making them hypertextual, mobile, and malleable.

This technological acceleration of cultural evolution, has a culmination of sorts in the postmodern condition.[6] With the end of modernity and the unifying project of the Enlightenment, our cultural condition is one of fluid and mobile signification. There is a sense of collapse where cultural systems that seek to finalise this or that aspect of reality, such as modernism, Marxism, or science, have suffered a deconstructive reappraisal. Instead of theoretical or stylistic purity, we find eclecticism, plurality, and ironic juxtaposition.

Cyberspace, hypermedia, and the transformation of traditional practices in all areas of culture all participate in this condition. The technology of simulation has made the textual base of culture virtual and fluid. This fluidity now conditions the sensibilities of those who develop within it to the point that, as Baudrillard has argued with respect to the media and advertising, what now counts as reality is what can be simulated. Mechanical mimesis, the technology of simulacra, a cultural movement whose beginnings were detected by Benjamin, has rendered the condition of post-industrial culture one of reproduction on the grand scale.[7] Presently, in what Lyotard calls the libidinal economy of post-industrial culture, this mimesis is imploding, rendering the present condition one of quotation and eclecticism.[8] Sign value, as Jameson has argued, has come to dominate both use and exchange value as the economic basis of society.[9] As a direct effect, human sensitivities and desires are more malleable, and hence are changing more rapidly than ever before. Hypermedia are now in primary schools and will soon be in the cradle. The generations that will develop within a technology of simulacra will experience a world where boundaries previously taken as fixed and patent will weaken and become more negotiable. The natural and the artificial, the original and the derivative, the real and the fictional, the spontaneous and the contrived will blend as never before. Some comments from Vaclav Havel touch on these themes:

> Today, many things indicate that we are going through a transitional period, when it seems that something is on its way out and something else is painfully being born . . . the distinguishing features

of such transitional periods are a mixing and blending . . . a tendency
to quote, to imitate and to amplify, rather than to state with
authority or integrate. New meaning is gradually born from the
encounter, or the intersection, of many different elements . . . this
state of mind or of the human world is called postmodernism. [10]

Postmodernism as a conceptual tool for understanding cultural change is
useful to the extent that developments in different areas can be shown to be
part of an underlying movement. A bridge between disciplines is formed if,
say, in the humanities and science such common patterns of change can be
found. In fact, as Charles Jencks and others have shown, in many areas
such shifts have been a feature of western culture for decades now.[11] They
have to do with the new fluidity and mobility of signification. They also
have to do with the debate between advocates of stylistic and theoretical
unification and advocates of pluralism.

Now the mixing and blending of book culture with hypermedia touches
on just these issues which, as George Landow points out, challenge
assumptions of ownership and authenticity, both of individual texts and of
the meta-narrative of disciplines as a whole.[12] Hypermedia also challenge
how texts are presently written, how they are read and edited, and how
critical reactions to them are developed. These practices are presently
oriented towards the values and sensitivities of the printed page. As
hypermedia appear in all these practices, cybernetically oriented
sensitivities and values will be created. Here, perhaps, is an example of the
intersection of many different elements that Havel has in mind. What new
meaning will be gradually born of this encounter cannot presently be
known. However, the encounter is certain to leave a trace in human
consciousness, having to do with what feels natural as a vehicle for
discourse, narrative, and criticism. This is not only a matter of cultural
theory but also something with very practical consequences.

Postmodernism and Practicalities

Postmodernism is not so much a condition as a direction. It is a cultural
shift that not only promotes change in the theory but also in the practice of
many disciplines. Changes to the textual basis of culture are part of this
shift towards a greater mobility and fluidity of texts. These changes will
perhaps be most keenly felt in the humanities because here the text is in
some sense more sacred than it is in, say, science. As media become
hypermedia they are ceasing to be localized ink on paper, but are
distributed and electronic. There is a shift from isolated linear texts to
interconnected web-like hypertexts. Libraries are less like storehouses and
more like nodes in an information retrieval system. There are
corresponding changes to how texts are produced and used. Books invite
systematic reading, although they can be explored and browsed. Hypertexts

on the other hand invite exploration, although they can, with effort, be systematically read. While books have readers whom the author has cast in the role of audience, hypertexts have users who are participants since they may also become authors, depending on how the system has been put together by its originators. Pedagogical texts are structured by teachers, hypertexts are structured by teachers and users together. As a result pedagogy shifts from instruction and memory to discovery and search skills. Competence which used to be assessed by the capacity for recall and critical analysis shifts towards performance and ironic collage as the essay becomes the composition.

This shift is not occurring in a political vacuum. In the United Kingdom we are still in an era of a massive and under-resourced increase in student numbers in higher education. Despite heroic efforts it has not been possible to maintain the quality of teaching nor of the resource infrastructure that supports it. While information technology is sometimes represented as a way to repair the damage it is just as, if not more, likely to be the means to make yet further bogus economies. More computers mean fewer teachers, distance learning via the Internet, lectures enhanced by hypermedia given to massive audiences dispersed in space and time, and distributed textual resources on a pay-to-use basis. All these things share in the logic of late capitalism. The theoretical vocabulary of post-Fordist economics applies to the Academy too. Not only corporations but also universities face 'downsizing' and a shrinking unit resource, the commodification of information and access to it, and performance-related pay based on quantitative indicators.

These trends already affect teaching, learning and how academics present their work to others. Although most lectures are still largely given by the traditional arrangement, where somebody speaks to others who are physically present, the thin but bright edge of the hypermedia wedge can already be seen. Lecture notes can be retrieved from a computer system, video projections appear on screens which may be linked to computers the other side of the globe. Conferences too now often involve a type of performance academia where animated data displays, videos, computer graphics, and sounds accompany or even comprise what it is that the lecturer has to say. Hypermedia are now tools for the communication of textual culture at the highest level.

At what might be called an entry level, students are encouraged to develop their writing skills helped by the reactions of those who teach them. But whose work is here in question? Texts are increasingly prepared and presented electronically. Wordprocessors have spelling and syntax checkers that work in real time and are customized to the idiosyncratic shortcomings of individual users. Texts can be written, edited, copied, enhanced, and circulated as never before. Bibliographic and reference materials come not just from reading lists, but from automated searches of databases using sophisticated tools. Locating, collating, and combining relevant materials have become electronically enhanced. This fluidity and mobility of texts and critical responses is part of the cut-and-paste culture of the Internet. If hypertextual scholarship promotes the reading of original texts, while speeding up and amplifying critical responses to them, then there has been a qualititative gain. If it does not, then the price of the transition to a new style of academic work appears to be a loss of quality to do with originality and individual responsibility.

If large, even exhaustive, lists of relevant references can be found with smart database tools then lecturers will increasingly find sources being quoted that they will not have read. Given the time to follow things up, this is an advantage rather than anything else. But as staff-to-student ratios slide, it will become more and more difficult to check whether items in bibliographies and references actually exist, let alone whether they have been correctly used or whether they have actually been read or not. But as for students, so for teachers. The resources of hypermedia scholarship work for everyone and if students use spelling and syntax checkers, and why should they not, then perhaps lecturers may expect cybernetic assistants who survey text for poor structure and plagiarism while at the same time checking the accuracy of bibliographies and references.

As hypermedia tools and practices take hold, they will inevitably change the sensitivities of lecturers and students to what counts as the textual basis of their subject. The book may well undergo something like the modulation of authenticity that Benjamin foresaw for works of art as mechanical means for reproduction took hold. As the cultural *milieu* is shaped by powerful tools and practices that radically accelerate the creation and distribution of meaning, this will create new values and sensitivities. The transition from books to hypermedia will profoundly effect what 'feels right' as a vehicle for textual culture.

Such transitions are happening all the time and are charged with value. For instance, when paperbacks first appeared they had a rather downmarket feel and there was quite a sharp reaction that this was somehow devaluing the status of the book. Now, after a generation or so of cultural conditioning, this feel is gone. The values involved in the coming trial of strength between book and electronic culture are equally charged. Already it is clear that hypermedia attract the same sorts of critical reactions that books do. Students will talk about how easy to use this hypertext is or how user-friendly that system feels. Similar critical responses to authorial styles cannot be far away.

Hypermedia are already well entrenched and with this comes a change in what Bourdieu calls the *habitus* of academic culture.[13] The *habitus* is a set of dispositions, tastes, practices and values that are developed, shared and transmitted by a community of practice. When there begins to be a feel, a distinctive set of values, to the new tools of a discipline, then a *habitus* has emerged. One way to track this is via the sense of personal value invested in the material resources of a discipline. The value placed on personal copies of beloved novels is clear, but the emotional significance of books that are actually textual tools can be under-rated. Their role in the rites of passage of academic life links them in a very deep way to personal identity. Such a lot can be invested in the tattered copy of Brown's *Freud and the Post-Freudians* or the compact, comforting, and densely annotated copy of Hart's *Organic Chemistry: A Short Course*, that were these books to be lost, an important part of the owner's history would go with them. Now, for all that they compact texts so wonderfully, could the shiny CD-ROM ever have the same emotional charge or homely feel? If it does this will be a signal that hypermedia will have become integrated into cultural transmission in a deep and significant way.

Again, there may well be a difference between disciplines here. In science and technology, the nature of their practice being what it is, hypermedia may fundamentally change what counts as the authoritative statement. Already, the proposal has been made that scientific research should not appear in paper journals, but instead be circulated on the Internet as a refereed discourse. This, it appears, would bring about an overnight transition to a post-Gutenberg era of scientific discourse.[14] There may indeed be something about science that lends itself to communication via hypermedia. Advances in physics or biology, although they may be expressed in formulae and diagrams, are often closely tied to dynamic images. Texts that can display these underlying images will offer a mode of communication that, as part of the postmodern challenge to boundaries and the blending of traditions, combines the scientific method with the textual traditions of the humanities.

The Nerve Bible, a work by the performance artist Laurie Anderson, begins and ends with the image of a burning book. Throughout the piece, a cascade of cyberspace icons pours from the vast on-stage screens, and even the written programme was thick with Internet and World Wide Web addresses. Anderson is sponsored by a US publishing house called Voyager. In the theatres where *The Nerve Bible* is presented, there are displays of Voyager's publications many of which are by authors with international academic reputations, like Marvin Minsky and Donald Norman. These publications cover music, the visual arts, history, biology, and psychology. All are on CD-ROM. What counts as the textual base of science and technology, albeit in popular form, is changing fast.

But these hypermedia and the academic mementoes mentioned above are secondary texts or textual tools, and predominantly scientific ones at that. What of the book itself, the primary textual vehicle of the humanities? Will this ancestral vehicle of textual culture be consumed in Anderson's transforming fire? Perhaps here the case is different; perhaps the book is fire-proof.

How It Feels

John Updike, to whom neither science nor technology is alien, celebrates the book in sharp and dismissive distinction to hypermedia. What he celebrates, however, is the book's aesthetics :

> . . . the charming little clothy box of the thing, the smell of the glue, even the print, which has its own beauty. There's something about the sensation of ink on paper that is in some sense a thing, a phenomenon rather than an epiphenomenon. I can't break the association of electronic trash with the computer screen. Words on the screen give the sense of just being another passing electronic wriggle.[15]

Now why is the book celebrated in this way? Obviously, books are beautiful in ways that hypermedia may never be, but why are screens felt to display mere passing electronic trash? Perhaps the stimulus for this dismissive reaction is a challenge to the *habitus* of the literary establishment. The *habitus* is not merely the private language of an inward-looking subculture; it bears signs of authority and power into the wider cultural arena. Possibly Updike and other celebrants of literary sensitivities feel that their *habitus* has the authority that Shelley gave to poets. For the unelected legislators of mankind, what feels right and beautiful does not so much *symbolise* what they do, it *is* what they do. The aesthetics of the book participate in the wider practice of literature, the disclosure of the human condition through narrative. The beauty of the covers has meaning within a narrative practice which normally entails a beginning, an end, and an effort, after felicity in between. Even typefaces have meaning. What is typographically appropriate for a romance by Scott may be quite wrong for a brutal, spare tale by Hemingway. The way books are encountered, what they present to the eye and mind together, has meaning within a larger practice of narrative.

Aesthetics are thus a pointer to fundamental questions. Will what lies beyond the book create new sensitivities and values concerning discourse? Will the advent of hypermedia bring new ways to present a narrative and to frame a critical response? If hypermedia are merely a means to transmit textual culture, and if that culture, especially its narrative elements, has an internal logic dictated by how the mind works, then the answer is no. Hypermedia may expand and change the *habitus* of literary culture, but nothing in the fundamental experience of a narrative will alter.

Time, space, and the human mind being what they are, narrative is a matter of structured progression. The challenge of hypermedia is said to lie in their web-like interconnectivity and dense cross-referencing. But how deep is this challenge really? From *Tristram Shandy* through *Ulysses* to *Catch 22* it is clear that well before the era of hypermedia literacy, books presented narratives in hypermedia fashion. The reverse case, while possible, is less interesting. Hypermedia are powerful means to enhance secondary textual resources, but to present a novel in hypertext form adds little to what the book already does and might even be a distraction.

Of course, it is not the advent of hypermedia alone that has raised the question of how technology will change textual practice and sensitivities. This question has been about for decades in education. Teachers and lecturers have long suspected that television has changed habits of attention and expectations about how an argument is presented and illustrated. Perhaps hypermedia are set to make similar changes in how the textual basis of a subject is encountered by learners and teachers alike. The skills of reading, for example, may change to reflect the habits of attention that develop in exploring hypermedia. Books, and textbooks in particular, may come to feel restrictive to students used to surfing the Internet. Part of the glamour of hypermedia stems from the participatory role of the user. Perhaps it is for this reason that the aesthetics of hypermedia, at present at least, are more functional, having to do with how elegantly or naturally the user is able to get from one part of the text to another. Eventually, merely reading a book may feel passive by comparison.

However, hypermedia can also appear bland and uniform, reflecting the constraints of the authorware rather than the subject being displayed. This problem can be aggravated if no extended passages are offered. Merely skipping between textbites can be oppressive if users are not able to add links of their own. Authors slip from authority to authoritarianism if they control too closely what secondary linkages are added to the primary text. This amounts to a form of thought control in comparison to which the homely virtues of the book seem both liberating and liberal.

Hypermedia seen in this light are almost parasitic, like jackals around a kill that the lions of deconstruction have already made. After Derrida chokes the narrative voice and Foucault attacks the text, what's left is yet further dismembered. But then, magically, it is re-membered with the electronic wizardry of hypermedia. The text is rebuilt as a hypertext with powerful ways of getting around the new structure. A remarkable transformation, but can the book as the vehicle for narrative survive such treatment?

Why the Book is Basic

Much depends on the book in question. Most books are not a vehicle for a literary narrative. Rather, they are reference works, textbooks, manuals, and lists. These are the tools and general *habitus* of literate culture. In the more specialized arena of the humanities, dictionaries, concordances, materials for language teaching, catalogues, and the like are powerfully amplified by being transformed into hypermedia. As such things are used earlier and earlier in intellectual development, so they will come to feel natural. A consequence of this internalization of technology, as McLuhan pointed out, is that consciousness changes. As the tools and practices of postmodern culture are internalized, so the sensitivities and values that are brought to a text will change.

Heidegger has explored the consequences of technology and concluded they are profound.[16] Human consciousness, he argues, has been transformed by the huge explosion of technology during the modern era. The world seen by the pre-Socratics is not where we live now. What to Heraclitus was an ever-flowing creative advance, we now experience as a standing resource for human action. Heidegger also considered how tools participate in the habitus of technological culture. Tools disappear from consciousness as they are naturalized, although they change it in the process. Heidegger distinguished the 'present-at-hand' from the 'ready-to-hand', identifying the former with what feels artificial and the latter with the natural and unconscious. So long as a tool is working properly, it disappears into the action for which it is being used. When it is unfamiliar or when it malfunctions, it reappears in consciousness.

When hypermedia tools disappear from consciousness in this way they will have undergone a McLuhanesque internalization. But what in the *habitus* of textual culture will have changed in the process? Will the book then feel un-natural, present-at-hand, an obstacle to really engaging with the text? This is much the way that hypermedia feel now to the dinosaurs of book culture. The question is, can there be a reversal such that books will come to feel the same way to the community of hypermedia scholarship that is so rapidly taking form?

The answer is no. Despite the radical claims made for hypermedia it is likely that only tool-like texts will undergo this assimilation into the *habitus* of hypermedia scholarship. Such texts will be enhanced by hypermedia since they lend themselves to the rapid shifts of view or the location of particular items that is their use-value. But books that offer a narrative or a sustained critical argument will not be enhanced. Linearity, for all that it may seem old fashioned, is a property of narrative and of consciousness, of Bergson's *dureé*.

Hypermedia will transform some bookish practices and will create some entirely new ones, but the effects, powerful as they may be, will not fundamentally change the book. This is because what counts in narrative is what the human mind does, not what technology can bring about. As we move into the era of hypermedia, what lies beyond the book will remain book-like. What constitutes a text will remain grounded in human capacities for producing and understanding discourse. Of course, as technology changes there will appear new ways to practise bookish traditions. As these develop, the human capacity for discourse will change accordingly. However, *pace* McLuhan, such change has limits. While the sense of what constitutes a narrative and a critical argument may be amplified here or modulated there, it will not be fundamentally altered.

Thus, overnight transitions as a result of hypermedia will only occur in specialized areas like scientific publishing, if they occur at all. Hypermedia will bring new tools and practices to certain communities of practice. But these communities and their culture are forming above rather than beyond the book. In a conservative but non-prescriptive way, the book in its present form will remain the foundation of the humanities. It is a cultural tool of resilient and enduring character, even though that character will be expressed in a different way as technology evolves. Many new modes of presenting texts will appear and many books will be transformed into hypermedia. Even so, the nature of narrative will not change. What the book already offers is a vehicle for this universal feature of human discourse at an appropriate level of technology. As a vehicle for the narrative voice, the book cannot be bettered.

Notes

1. J. Baudrillard, *The Ecstacy of Communication* translated by Bernard and Caroline Schutze, edited by Sylvére Lotringer (New York: Semiotext(e), 1988).
2. M. McLuhan, *The Gutenberg Galaxy* (London: Routledge and Keegan Paul, 1962), 42 *et seq.*
3. For recent and accessible contributions to this area, see J. Kingdon, *Self-made Man and His Undoing* (London: Simon and Schuster, 1993) or, slightly more technically, B. Goodwin, *How the Leopard Changed its Spots: The Evolution of Complexity* (London: Weidenfeld and Nicolson, 1994).
4. For a very broad but accessible account see U. Maturana, and F. Varela, *The Tree of Knowledge: The Biological Roots of Human Understanding* (Boston: Shambala, 1987). A more specialized treatment is C. Sinha, *Language and Representation: A Socio-naturalistic Approach to Human Development* (Hemel Hempstead: Harvester, 1988).
5. C. Tudge, 'Are Human Beings Still Evolving? *New Scientist*, 15 September 1988, 70-71.
6. Of the huge number of sources on postmodernism, recommended starting points are: C. Jencks, (ed.) *The Postmodern Reader* (London: Academy Editions, 1992); J.-F. Lyotard, *The Postmodern Condition: A Report on Knowledge* (Manchester: Manchester University Press, 1984); and D. Harvey, *The Condition of Postmodernity* (Oxford: Blackwell, 1990).
7. Benjamin's best known statement on this is his essay 'The Work of Art in the Age of Mechanical Reproduction'. It can be found on pages 219-253 of his *Illuminations*, translated by H. Zohn, (Glasgow: Fontana, 1979).

8. J.-F. Lyotard, *Libidinal Economy* translated by Ian Hamilton Grant (Bloomington: Indiana University Press, 1993). Originally published as *Economie Libidinale* (Paris: Editions Minut, 1974).

9. F. Jameson, 'Postmodernism, or the Cultural Logic of Late Capitalism' *New Left Review*, 146, 53-93.

10. This quotation comes from a speech given by Vaclav Havel on being awarded the liberty medal in Philadelphia on 4 July, 1994. It is reprinted in *Resurgence*, 169,1995.

11. C. Jencks, 'The Postmodern Agenda' in *The Postmodern Reader*, ed. Charles Jencks, (London: Academy Editions, 1992).

12. G. Landow, *Hypertext: The Convergence of Contemporary Critical Theory and Technology* (London: Johns Hopkins University Press, 1992).

13. P. Bourdieu, *The Logic of Practice* translated by Richard Nice (Cambridge: Polity Press, 1990). Bourdieu discusses the *habitus* of academic culture in *Homo Academicus*, translated by Peter Collier, (Cambridge: Polity Press, 1984).

14. S. Harnad, 'Post-Gutenberg Galaxy Wars' *Times Higher Educational Supplement*, 12 May 1995.

15. This quotation is from an article entitled 'Fictions, Facts and the Future' by D. Max, which appeared in the supplement to the *Guardian*, 3 January 1995, 12-13.

16. M. Heidegger, *The Question Concerning Technology, and Other Essays* translated by William Lovitt (London: Harper and Row, 1977). For an informal account of Heidegger's views on tools see chapter 3 of T. Winograd and F. Flores, *Understanding Computers and Cognition* (New Jersey: Ablex, 1986).

Re-Viewing the Film (Studies) Text

Michael Allen
School of English and American Studies
University of East Anglia

As the title suggests, I have a double agenda in writing this paper: to examine the potential effects of multimedia on the film text, and to examine the potential effects of multimedia on the writing of the Film Studies text. I hope to investigate several related areas: the elements which go to make up the identity of the various audio-visual texts; the nature of the viewing experience; questions of Film Studies methodology, including the place of the written word, archiving, and statistics; whether multimedia techniques are suitable for all types of Film Study. My achievement, if any, will probably be to raise far more questions than I answer. But, perhaps, this befits a field which has been, and which shows no signs of being other than, one in continual turmoil and change.

I want first to consider the relationship between the various audio-visual media, film, TV, and video (within which we should now include multimedia). According to John Ellis in *Visible Fictions*:

> Cinema, broadcast TV, and non-broadcast video are often gathered together under one heading: the audio-visual. This definition elides much that is different about the three forms. They have a common concern with images and sounds, but each has different visual and audible materialities. The cinema image is photographic; the video image electronic. These distinctions bring with them a series of different attentions to the images and sounds, and therefore a rather different set of possibilities of representations.[1]

To investigate this question of where multimedia might fit into this overall field, we should consider the nature of the main elements which constitute the viewing experiences of these media.

Cinema is generally perceived to be a *recorded* rather than a live text. By that I mean that it is seen as representing past events, whether real or fictional, rather than those existing in the actual present. Obviously, this is largely due to the fact that the image has to be recorded on to celluloid and sound-strip, which then have to be processed into the finished work. Only then is the text ready to be viewed by an audience. Viewing of this text generally takes place in very low-light or darkened circumstances. Cinema presents the viewer with a huge image (even in the smallest screen of a modern multiplex centre); one which has to be looked up to from a physically subservient position (especially if you are in the front row). The cinema image casts a luminous light out from the screen. Images shimmer and glow due to the effect of light beams hitting the glass particles of which the screen is physically constituted. Films now have an enveloping sound quality, thanks to the Dolby stereo or even quadraphonic surround-sound which is a standard part of the modern cinema playback system.

Cinema displays its wares to what is, almost invariably, a captive audience; one can leave the room, but it is a brave and inconvenient move to make, especially from the centre of the seating row. As a result, the viewing circumstances tend to demand unqualified attention and concentration. This unqualified attention is what John Ellis refers to as The Gaze, and is something I will return to in more detail later.

In contrast, TV is perceived to be largely live rather than recorded, even though a significant percentage of its product actually isn't live these days. It is perceived to offer a representation of a present event rather than one which has existed in the past. Television is generally viewed in the lightened circumstances of a living room. Lighting conditions, whether by main light or table lamp, are controllable by the viewer. It presents the viewer with a small image; even at its largest about two feet square. The viewer can, at any time, adjust the brightness and contrast quality of the image, as well as the sound level. The viewer always has elementary control over the material to be displayed on the screen, in the sense that, at any moment, he or she can switch channels and view a radically different text. Television, as Ellis has argued, also relies upon an emphasised sound component to carry more of the narrative weight than the cinematic film does (which relies more on the image). This is, in some sense, paradoxical, as television sets generally have a quite degraded sound quality, due to the technical inferiority of their in-built loudspeakers.

Television plays to a non-captive audience which is free to come and go as it pleases. It is generally on for several hours every day, displaying its material whether its audience is paying attention or not. This intermittent attention is what Ellis refers to as The Glance:

> Gazing is the constituent activity of cinema. Broadcast TV demands
> a rather different kind of looking: that of the glance. Gazing at the
> TV is a sign of intensity of attention that is usually considered
> slightly inappropriate to the medium.[2]

Video occupies a middle ground between cinema and television. It is like TV in terms of its image and sound quality, unsurprisingly, considering that video is almost always displayed on a TV screen. If anything, however, video presents an even more degraded quality, certainly in the visual sense. However, like cinema, video is perceived, explicitly, to be recorded rather than live. Indeed, that is its very *raison d'être* – it is used to record material and play it back at a later time. And, like TV, it allows the viewer complete controllability over the display of its material, via the ubiquitous remote control handset.

Cinema, as a site of reception, offers a narrative incentive and incitement to attend a public arena. TV and video offer to import their products into your private space. You don't go to them, they comes to you; ceaselessly. As a result, the spectator produces a different series of identifications with the images and figures in the different media. Identification is intense in terms of cinema, less so with TV and video, which do not so completely replace the viewer's real-life context. A number of writers on film have observed the similarity of the film viewing experience to dreaming.[3] They concentrate on the passivity of the film viewing experience, mentally active but physically inactive; a passivity and inactivity intensified by the particular viewing circumstances of a two-hour film. In this state, the spectator is unable to influence the passage of the film, and it has been argued that a fantasy of helplessness is essential to the effect of the narrative drive.

The particular physical set-up of conventional film viewing intensifies this fantasy state. For Christian Metz:

> During the projection the camera is absent, but it has a representative consisting of another apparatus, called precisely a "projector". An apparatus the spectator has behind him, *at the back of his head*, that is, precisely where fantasy locates the focus of all vision.[4]

While for Jean-Louis Baudry:

> No doubt the darkened room and the screen bordered with black like a letter of condolence already present privileged conditions of effectiveness – no exchange, no circulation, no communication with the outside. Projection and reflection take place in a closed space, and those who remain there, whether they know it or not (but they do not), find themselves chained, captured, or captivated.[5]

'Chained', 'captured' and 'captivated' are evocative terms which register the particular psychic effect film viewing can have upon us.

Cinema offers a one-off, self-contained product, which lasts two or three hours and then ends. We know it ends, because we are shepherded away from the site of its reception, the cinema auditorium. The theatre is then re-filled with another audience of like-minded spectators, who then experience exactly the same viewing experience. In comparison, TV offers a never-ending flow of product in relatively discrete segments: small sequential unities of images and sounds. These segments are organized into groups, which are either simply cumulative, as in the case of advert breaks or magazine-type programmes, or have some kind of repetitive or sequential connection, as in the case of serials or soap operas. The possible exception to this is the case of feature films shown on TV, or TV-made films, which are one-off, hermetically sealed texts, existing within an entertainment format which possesses a completely different logic. Even here, however, the feature length film text might be split into sections by advertisement breaks. Each of these breaks interrupt the fiction and the fantasy of the film work in a way never experienced by the audience in the movie theatre.

If, at long last, I can bring multimedia into the argument, I would suggest that audio-visual material presented on computer operates in an area somewhere between these various positions. It usually takes place in a light environment, on a small screen like television, but asks for the sustained attention and concentration typical of the cinema. But it also offers degrees of control and power over the machine similar to the video image. The computer holds a collection of discrete texts—text files, still images, movie clips—which are brought into various combinations by the options offered by the particular program being used. The texts are of varying length. A written text might take hours to read properly, whereas a still image or movie clip might take only seconds to view. This discrepancy in length between the various text types, and the consequent discrepancy in the degree of effort and commitment required in reception, are characteristics peculiar to multimedia and hypertext, the implications of which have not properly been thought out to date. There is a demand on the part of the user to shift 'reception-mode' quite radically and quite rapidly as a multimedia hypertext program is explored. The processes of multimedia and hypertext produce a strange hybrid form. We know that the material is already 'in there', stored on the computer's hard disk or CD-ROM, and therefore predictable. But this material becomes, in a sense, live, and unpredictable in the actual event of accessing it in particular combinations of text, movies, pictures, and sounds. Each combination of texts, each user-experience, is, in theory at least, unique.

Perhaps the magic, if I can use such an evocative term, of sound and image on the computer is that it is *somewhere it shouldn't be.* It is not simply that the computer cannot be seen as a site of entertainment. We have all been forced to come to terms with the irritating reality of computer games, with their cartoon images and repetitive movements. But exactly because of this identification with the trivial and banal, it is perhaps still difficult to accept the computer as the potential site of 'adult', sophisticated, high-quality entertainment. To see 'real people', moving and speaking in miniature on a computer screen, *is* genuinely magical.

In this, incidentally, there is a harking back to the earliest days of cinema. When the first screen-projected films were shown to the first audiences, they had the awesome effect of the new and the inexplicable. Giant moving objects from real life appeared before the audiences' eyes: huge trains rushed straight towards those sitting in their Nickelodeon seats,[6] a gesticulating man advanced towards the camera into extreme close-up, before opening his mouth so that it filled the entire screen before 'eating' the camera and camera operator.[7]

There is a strange 'coming-full-circle' involved in considering the similarities between the first motion picture machines, developed at the end of the nineteenth century, and the latest multimedia workstations, in the sense that the spectator of the earliest films had a measure of control over the material they were viewing which is very like that of the modern multimedia user. The Kinetoscope spectator paid his or her 10 cents, and purchased the opportunity to turn a handle on the side of the machine casing. This put in motion the loop of film within and displayed a simple scene—a music-hall act, or one scene of a multi-scene biblical epic—through a viewfinder. Only one person could view this brief filmstrip at any one time. The multimedia workstation similarly offers its solo user the opportunity to choose to view a short video clip. That clip can be played, paused, restarted, and replayed using simple controls. The length of the moving material being viewed is, in both cases, technologically determined: by the length of film strip and crude mechanism in the case of the Kinetoscope, and by hard-disk storage space and processor speed in the case of Quicktime clips on a computer monitor.

If we now focus the argument down to a specific issue, that of viewing cinema films on the other media, we have to consider a complex social and economic matrix which has resulted in the acceptance of the substantially degraded technical quality of the film as it appears on TV. Lip service is paid to quality, almost as if a guilty voice is speaking, when videodisk is volunteered as a breathtaking technical improvement which will bring the authenticity of the cinema experience into your home. Nothing of the kind. The cinema image, in terms of quality, still wins hands down. What we have been seeing over the past couple of decades, therefore, is a kind of regression. The film industry, having poured time, money, and effort into perfecting the quality of the cinematic image and the veracity of the sound reproduction, has been forced to see that quality substantially compromised for largely economic reasons. The bottom line is that the degraded quality of the film image on video or TV is has become accepted because of a combination of economic and social factors.

Issues of quality are often ignored in discussions of multimedia, which tend to assume that films can be transferred to TV or video with little or no real problem. The fact that, for economic rather than aesthetic reasons, the majority of people now see films on TV or video rather than in the cinema indicates the success of the strategy and its acceptance in the popular mind. If it comes to a showdown between image/sound quality and ease of access, we'll take the latter most times out of ten. This situation, I think, makes acceptance of the *even lower* quality of sound and image produced by multimedia possible.

But the technological advances in multimedia have their positive side as well, and prompt several further questions. Firstly, should we really be concerned about this historical development? After all, we lost something when illuminated manuscripts gave way to Caxton's printing press, but something was also gained in the process: quality for accessibility, to put it crudely. And, in fact, we might gain far more—a new art form. We could see, for example, audio-visual works which offer multiple narrative trajectories, rather than the one, linear trajectory of classical film. (These are already being considered, though more in the product area of interactive games than conventional cinema.)[8] And we will certainly see a new textual form develop which consciously mixes together images, both still and moving, with written text to produce a hybrid form. Each medium would then be able to do what it does best, rather than also try to do what it is inadequate at portraying (movement in the case of stills, interior thought in the case of film, and actual sound and vision in the case of the written word).

The second thought is that these developments have serious implications for the study of film, consideration of which will now form the second half of this article.

Raymond Bellour has observed:

the special difficulties which very often make it impossible to obtain the film in the material sense or the proper conditions to constitute it into a text, i.e. the editing table or the projector with freeze-frame facility. These difficulties are still enormous: they are very often discouraging, and go a long way to explaining the comparative backwardness of film studies. However, one can imagine, if still only hypothetically, that one day, at the price of a few changes, the film will find something that is hard to express, a status analogous to that of the book or rather that of the gramophone record with respect to the concert. If film studies are still done then, they will undoubtedly be more numerous, more imaginative, more accurate and above all more enjoyable than the ones we carry out in fear and trembling, threatened continually with dispossession of the object.[9]

In the Good Old Days of Film Studies, a film was viewed in a darkened theatre in the same way as it would have been as an entertainment in the cinema—in Film Studies, the two experiences are often very different!—with members of the audience scribbling notes blind on to pieces of paper. The student then scurried off to his or her desk, to convert the illegible notes into a stunning piece of incisive criticism, complete with long descriptive passages to compensate for the absence of the film. If the student was both dedicated and technical enough, he or she might possibly include a few photos to represent significant points in the sequence being analysed. The trouble is, the Good Old Days are pretty much still with us. This is very much how Film Studies is still being taught. Videotape has altered the situation slightly, but mostly in terms of providing cheaper and more flexible viewing possibilities. There is usually only one copy of the video in circulation, so that not much is solved in terms of one-to-one access.

At the moment of critical writing (and reading), the film itself is an Absent Text—it is not present in any real way in the words on the page. It has only a phantom presence, in the descriptive passages which attempt to recreate the sensations of light, movement, colour, and sound which make up the original film text. The reader depends upon the accuracy of the writer's language to recreate imaginatively the absent text in his own mind.

Multimedia—with its Quicktime Movies or Video for Windows technology—promises to change this situation by allowing the direct quotation of film clips within the written text. For the first time the film text can be made manifest at the time of critical unfolding. The reader can play the movie material, read the critical point, replay the movie material, and so on as many times as desired. Moreover, multimedia programs tend to offer a range of filmic devices—zooms, fades, wipes, and so on—as part of their construction syntax. So, for the first time, writers on film can use something of the same language as the text to which they are referring. Even in a general sense, this increases the student's awareness of the processes taking place in the original film text.

Such an advance has its potential downside. The evocative description of the Absent Film Text, focused in its attention to detail and sensitive in its use of language, has a particular beauty, and effect, all of its own. 'Good' Film Studies writing, at least in certain areas of the field, has always succeeded by drawing attention to significant detail and attempts to evoke the emotional layers of the text. (Emotion is a vastly under-rated aspect of the film text. Most film narratives are driven by the emotional relationships between their characters and depend upon emotional reaction from the spectator for their final effect.) Relinquishing that duty by allowing the film clip to describe itself, in effect, introduces the possibility for a certain 'looseness', a possible inexactitude. The reader might not see in the clip what the writer has seen and now wants to convey to the reader. The reader might, simply, just not 'get it'. In this case the film clip, although instantly and endlessly re-playable, still will not get the point across. The point, in effect, might just be lost.

Of course, Film Studies writing will not be either/or. There will not be a stubborn enclave of traditionalists, refusing all technical aid in their writing and insisting that they carry on producing long, mellifluous, descriptive passages. And, conversely, all Film Studies writing will not be in the new hi-tech multimedia hypertext form. Furthermore, in any work produced using hypertext technology, there will need to be some relationship between the writing and the visual material. Embedded buttons will carefully control the playback of the movie clips, isolating certain sections, certain gestures, certain movements. Attention will then be thrown back upon the writing, for the essential analytical point to be made.

I think the important point to be made here is that the possibilities being opened up by the advent of multimedia technologies in the Film Studies arena will significantly change the way Film Studies writing will be conceived. The rules for this relationship between written word and moving picture have yet to be formulated. And in this lies the future potential, and excitement, for Film Studies as a discipline.

There are other implications for Film Studies. Access to the films themselves, certainly in terms of obtaining rare copies from reluctant archives, has always been a major problem for students of the medium. Computer technologies offer the possibility of revolution in the area of film archiving and access to texts. Digitized electronic copies can be made to preserve the often fragile original. Access can be gained via the Internet to archives across the other side of the world. The hidden riches of obscure archives can be made available to the film students of the world. However, the transfer of film material into digital form is prohibitively expensive; an impossible dream for even the most affluent archive. Moreover, there is a political angle to this question which will become foregrounded with the increased presence of the new technologies in the Film Studies field as a whole. An archive which holds the only known copy of a rare film in its vaults holds a certain power in the market-place. Often the very survival of the archive depends upon the 'clout' provided by such treasures. Allowing anyone and everyone to have easy access to that text destroys that position. The whole economic, political, and conceptual makeup of the archiving network would have to change for this to take place. Not likely to happen in our lifetime.

Finally, on a specialist point: the computer's infamous number-crunching abilities also make it ideal for Statistical Style Analysis. Statistical Style Analysis is a minority area of Film Studies work, in which the input of substantial facts and figures about a film text (shot lengths, framings, frequencies of staging, and so on) allows that text to be interpreted for its stylistic distinctiveness via its statistical information. The computer can quickly sift through and organize this mass of data in revealing ways, possibly even illustrating the results in a graph. Computer technology can allow a text to be seen in a radically different way. It can take on a new shape, and this shape can literally present hidden information and ideas to the eye—a certain spread of shot lengths, or sudden strange changes in framing strategies. Such textual 'pressure points' are often hidden from view by the relentless forward movement of the film in normal viewing circumstances. This 'making strange' reveals these textual intensities by translating the text into an alien form which strips away the 'noise' of temporal and linear viewing to reveal the pure structure and form.

All of these are substantial advances, holding forth the possibility of transforming Film Studies as a discipline. Perhaps the fundamental question which these new developments raise is the very identity of the film text itself. Exactly what does it consist of? What exactly is being addressed in the critical work? The answer, crudely, is that it depends upon the style of analysis being conducted. The Film Studies text is many different things to many different writers. To the 'old generation' film writer, the film is an entity which elicits emotional responses from its spectator. It is the purpose of the writing to describe and evoke these responses, so that the text, as a thing of pleasure in the familiar sense of the word, is adequately conveyed. To the close textual analyst, it is a body of movements, stagings, details, all of which require the utmost attention and scrutiny if the full richness of the text is to be extracted via the analytical process. To the statistical style analyst, the text is a collection of facts and figures: exact shot length, precise framing definitions, frequencies of occurrence, and so on, which can be collated and interpreted to understand stylistic distinctions, studio styles, historical parameters. To the Reception Theorist, who studies the position of the film text in the market-place itself—who saw it and why; how the film was marketed; how it is culturally positioned—the film text as a text in itself is of less interest than the 'text' which is created by the film itself acting as a nexus for wider social phenomena. In this instance, the actual film text can almost disappear. It is the meta-discourse which is the more important.

Multimedia is currently a 'hot property'. It is being presented as the saviour of education, revolutionizing the study-place, bringing information to the fingertips and transforming ways of thinking. So much may indeed be true, and I would certainly hesitate to counter-argue the general point. But, in terms of Film Studies at least, the delights and potentials offered by multimedia may not be suitable for every type of Film Studies approach. The hyping of it, and the resultant peer pressure produced by this, might encourage certain kinds of study to the detriment of others. Areas which might not automatically benefit from a multimedia approach include narrative structure, reception studies, and historical studies.

Indeed, the use of multimedia and hypertext makes certain film studies investigations—such as lighting strategies used by a certain studio, or the precise differences between colour stocks—very difficult to assess by studying such a small and technically degraded image. What it does obviously offer to transform is the area of close analysis: taking a small section of film text and opening it to the concentrated scrutiny of its formal qualities. In this instance, the immediate, direct, and precisely controllable quotation of the film text itself can only be seen as a significant development.

But even here, we must be cautious. We must be sure of what it is that is allowing the analysis to be formulated in this particular way. In *S/Z*, Roland Barthes defines the *lexia* as:

> a series of brief, contiguous fragments, which we shall call *lexias*, since they are units of reading. This cutting up, admittedly, will be arbitrary in the extreme; it will imply no methodological responsibility, since it will bear on the signified. The *lexia* will include sometimes a few words, sometimes several sentences; it will be a matter of convenience: it will suffice that the *lexia* be the best possible space in which we can observe meanings; its dimension, empirically determined, estimated, will depend on the density of connotations, variable according to the moments of the text: all we require is that each *lexia* should have at most three or four meanings to be enumerated.[10]

The *lexia* therefore, while in some ways capricious, is almost wholly produced by an intellectual process, which determines where any one *lexia* begins and ends. The possible difference with multimedia approaches to the close analysis of film texts is that the available technology can partially determine the definition of the film *lexia*. In order to produce a computerized sequence of film, split into its *lexias* separately stored onto computer, several distinct operations have to be performed. Firstly, the original capture of the film clip on to the computer, via special sound and video boards. This is done in real time, and creates an immediate problem in the size of the captured clip, which can be tens of megabytes for even a short sequence. Storage limitation can predetermine the length of the film sequence we decide to analyse. Secondly, the full clip needs to be separated into its separate *lexias*. Each lexia will need converting into a new file, which, again, will take another period of time to produce even a short clip. Thirdly, and finally, these *lexias* have to be incorporated into the critical writing. I think that in a real sense, here, the technology is at least influencing, if not overtly determining, the definition of the *lexia*. This process, significantly, takes students several times longer to produce a finished piece of work than does traditional essay-writing.

An immediate effect of this—and this has actually happened at the University of East Anglia—is that a student might decide that some of this work is not worth its final effect, and will drop it from the study, adapting his or her argument accordingly. In this sense, the technology might actually be seen to be inhibiting the intellectual content of the finished work rather than aiding or even liberating it.

In spite of all the negative things I have said, I think that the magic of seeing what appears to be the impossible—a moving, audible film image on a computer screen—should not be underestimated. It provokes the same kind of enthusiasm for use which the earliest films caused. As with early cinema, there is a danger of foregrounding the technology over the films. But in spite of these reservations, multimedia technology can make significant, even revolutionary, changes to the study of the film text. We must just realize that it can't do everything better. Some things might be better done the old way. The relationship of the audio-visual material to the written text is complex and hasn't yet been satisfactorily considered. What proportion of the argument should be carried by the writing and what proportion by the film material? To what extent do you let the film material 'describe itself', while still presenting a coherent written argument? The new multimedia Film Studies text will have to formulate a new balance, new dialogues, between its various parts, deciding which element performs which work. In good time, these practices will become established and become second nature, like essay writing. In the interim, however, uncertainty and confusion can often be the result. But, then, so it is with any revolution worthy of the name.

1. John Ellis, *Visible Fictions* (London, Boston and Henley: Routledge and Kegan Paul, 1982), 38.
2. Ibid. 137.
3. See, for example, Ralph Stephenson, and J. R. Debrix, *The Cinema as Art* (Hammondsworth: Penguin Books, 1965); David Bordwell, *Narration and the Fiction Film* (London: Methuen, 1985).
4. Christian Metz, Christian, 'The Imaginary Signifier', *Screen* 16:2 (1975), 52.
5. Jean Louis Baudry, 'Ideological Effects of the Basic Cinematographic Apparatus', *Film Quarterly*, 28:2 (1974), 44.
6. *Train Entering a Station*, filmed by the Lumière Brothers in 1895, in which a steam train approaches a station platform at an angle from the right background to left foreground. People disembark and others climb aboard.
7. *The Big Swallow* (1901), in which a man becomes irate at being filmed, and approaches the camera to extreme close-up, until his open mouth covers the lens of the camera. A second, trick, shot shows the cameraman 'falling into the man's mouth'. A third shot shows the man pulling back into mid-shot, chewing with glee.
8. See the essay by Andrew Gibson, 'Interactive Fiction and Narrative Space', in this volume.
9. Raymond Bellour, 'The Unattainable Text', *Screen* 16:2 (1975), 19.
10. Roland Barthes, *S/Z* Trans. Richard Miller (London: Cape, 1975).

The Web, Semiotics, and History: Samuel Delany's Imagined Worlds

Laura Chernaik
Department of American and Canadian Studies
University of Nottingham

This paper is an analysis of an SF novel, *Stars In My Pockets Like Grains Of Sand*,[1] by the prominent gay Black American SF writer, Samuel Delany. Delany has been writing and publishing popular, theoretically sophisticated SF since the 1960s and has also, for much of his career, written articles and books on both SF theory and cultural studies. Delany is a deeply political writer, and at the same time, one concerned with language and genre. Delany's text displaces the economic and social form which is dominant in the developed world today, transnational capitalism, into a fictive, imagined universe, described as a multiplanetary economy. As in our world, the multiplanetary economy of the fictive universe has recurrent economic, social, and political crises. However, unlike our world, where a single economic system is perhaps becoming hegemonic, and where, contrary to the hopes many of us had in the 1960s and 1970s, there is now a backlash against alternative ways of living, and a return to the promotion and enforcement of norms, Delany's fictive universe contains a variety of social, economic and political structures, with different structures and ways of living dominant on each planet and planetary association. There are three political groupings which struggle for hegemony in the multiplanetary economy of *Stars*: the Web, the Sygn, and the Family. Each has its own members who, in their material, social, and spatial practices, build up different institutions and ways of living, distributed across the many inhabited worlds of the imagined universe. The Web is an information technology conglomerate; the Sygn is a network of multi-species affinity groups, displacing itself from world to world; the Family, as its name suggests, is a group whose members believe that there is only one true model for sociality, based on nuclear units in which reproductive one-species heterosexuality is normative. Delany's way of writing about each of these three discourses focuses on the importance, and significance, of history and politics.

A discourse is something which involves, which is made up of, both 'written' texts and social texts; both books, computer programs, the Internet, and so forth, and also institutions and human actions. As my comparison here suggests, I do not think that the new information technologies necessarily, in themselves, move us 'beyond the book'. As *information*, as coded, as written, information technologies can be analysed using the now-familiar tools of structuralism, poststructuralism, deconstruction, and postmodernism. If 'the book' is modern and 'information technology' postmodern, it is not because each technology is differently characterized as text. In what then does the difference lie? Information technology, I would argue, is a part, an important part, of one of the dominant discourses in Western, postmodern societies. As Donna Haraway argues, postmodern societies have seen a shift away from traditional constructions of identity, traditional working patterns, and traditional ways of conceptualizing the world.[2] One of the new concepts dominant in our postmodern societies is the notion of *command-control-communication-intelligence* (C3I). This notion, first developed in the military, is extensively used in both information science and biological science. However, I would argue that the significance of C3I, as a useful concept, lies in the way that it enables certain kinds of arguments, certain kinds of connections. It doesn't really matter whether or not C3I is a different kind of coding, a different kind of writing to that which was common previously. And, I would also argue, the best way to map out and explain these connections is in the traditional form of the book or article, a long prose work which gives one the space and the structure to develop a sustained argument and/or to describe something in sufficient detail to constitute a 'thick description'.[3] In many ways, narrative fiction, like narrative history and anthropologies, is as sucessful as—and sometimes more successful than—works which use non-narrative logics to show, in detail, these kind of historical connections.

Information technology, in *Stars*, is not just the source of an analytically suggestive metaphorics; information technology is itself the object of Delany's historical and political analysis. Information technology is represented as part, indeed a central part, of the imagined universe's political and economic workings. Delany is a Marxist, and he draws on neo-Marxist analyses of transnationalism in describing this fictional universe. Like, for example, David Harvey,[4] or Mike Davis,[5] Delany analyses transnationalism in Regulation School terms, theorizing it in terms of accumulation, rather than looking separately at production, consumption, and reproduction. Delany deals with transnationalism as a spatial practice, addressing the ways in which transnational capitalism, as a material practice, acts on and in space. He addresses the ways in which spatial practices are also, at the same time, spatial concepts, spatial ways of thinking. The widely separated planets of the imagined universe are linked in a common political and economic structure: one in which the three institutions, the Sygn, the Web, and the Family, strive for dominance. The Web's material basis is information technology: it manages and maintains 'General Information' satellites as well as providing an infrastructure of politicians, civil servants, researchers, and affiliated workers. These affiliates might be businessmen or women, drawn in to the plots of the Web 'spiders' like the businessmen in Britain who recently exposed the Matrix Churchill affair, or they might be 'deniable' Web agents. In this way, information technology is seen as irreducibly political, an essential part of the history and politics of the imagined universe, and, by implication, our own world.

My analysis of Delany's SF text addresses the ways in which, as well as drawing on neo-Marxism, Delany also draws on and addresses feminist theory, gay and lesbian theory, poststructuralism, and postmodernist narrative theory. When Delany addresses transnationalism as a material practice, in this work, he looks at the ways in which transnationalism produces species difference, race, gender, and sexuality as well as class.

This imagined future universe is not a utopia. *Stars* opens on an isolated planet, Rhyonon. The first part of the novel, 'A World Apart', tells the story of a man, Korga, who becomes a slave. Rhyonon, the planet, destroys itself in a cataclysm, a 'cultural fugue', one of the economic, cultural, and, of course, military crises to which life is subject, in this fictional world as well as our own. By a fluke, Korga, the slave, is the only survivor; he is rescued by the Web. The title of the first part of the novel is undecidable: it has two meanings. Rhyonon, the planet from which Korga comes, is a world apart; a slave society, with, in addition, a gender structure which, although familiar to a mundane reader, is unusual in the imagined universe of *Stars*. And Korga, the hero of the first part, is a world apart from Marq, the narrator of the rest of the novel. It is the Net which brings Korga and Marq together.

The Net, the institution which is in charge of information in this imagined universe, is frequently referred to, in the words of the novel, as the 'agency'. As the term 'agency' (a slang term for the CIA) suggests, the Web is, like the CIA, KGB, MI5, and so on, a dangerous, powerful, and, to say the least, not very nice, institution. Thus the Web officials are called 'spiders' by the other characters: Marq's boss is described as 'the Black Widow'. The Web both maintains a system of satellites orbiting every inhabited world which will agree to offer its citizens access to GI, General Information, and also compiles information on a vast range of subjects and objects. Thus, the Black Widow, Marq's boss, introduces him to Korga, his perfect object of desire. And, unlike computer dating agencies in our world, this one works: the two men fall in love.

Korga came from an isolated planet, but Marq comes from Velm, a world which is aligned to the Sygn. This word Sygn is spelled with a 'y', as if the imagined universe of *Stars* were the future of our universe, and, in the intervening time, English had become Arachnia and 'sign' had become 'sygn'. The word 'sygn' thus suggests displacement. And also, as, perhaps a variant on sign, the English word, it alludes to semiotics. And, indeed, the sygn, as an institution and an ideology, stresses interpretation.

In Delany's *Stars* transnationalism is explicitly linked to both displacement and dissemination. One of the most characteristic techniques used in SF is something usually referred to as 'the literalization of metaphor'. In *Stars*, Delany literalizes the metaphors of displacement and dissemination: the Sygn is quite literally displaced and disseminated, moving from world to world, spreading across the imagined universe. This literalization is also, of course, a spatialization. The spatialization of the metaphors of 'dissemination' and 'displacement' makes possible a particular view of history. Unlike many contemporary theorists, for whom deconstruction, as well as many radical poststructuralist and postmodernist theories, is considered to be in opposition to a historical and even a political approach to the text (or for whom, at the very least, a bridge between a historical approach and many radical poststructuralist, postmodernist, and deconstructive approaches is seen as difficult) Delany explicitly links the Sygn, the discourse in which semiotics and deconstruction are combined, with an approach in which history is seen as desperately important.

Delany, as a postmodern but narrative writer, is interested in the ways that history can be conceptualized; in the ways that history can be written. Delany is concerned both with the local, with local histories as such, and with the conceptual formation, local/global. Many leftist postmodernists and feminist theorists have argued that a materialist theory must shift between local and global, resisting both the seduction of detail and the temptation to systematize. Delany refers to this, in a typically parodic, self-referential manner, when Marq Dyeth says of the Sygn, the second of these institutions, that it is characteristically interested in the 'local histories of local spaces'. Marq says to another character (the passage is dialogue, an extract from a long speech):

> One of the Sygn's most widely spread tenets (and like everything else in the Sygn dogma, it, too, no matter how wide, does not obtain everywhere) is that history is what is outside, in both time and space, the current moment of home. And without history, there is no home. A second tenet that usually (though, like all else, not always) goes along with the first: when you go to a new world, all you can take of your home is its history. And if you are a woman, your choice is to take it knowingly and be its (and your new home's) silent friend, or to take it unknowingly and be its (and your new home's) loud slave.

And 'slave' is one of those words in Arachnia that, amidst a flurry of sexual suggestions, strongly connotes the least pleasant aspects of 'master'. (Delany, p. 105)

The Sygn's is a radically non-universalizing dogma, appropriate for a non-unitary subject. Delany's starting point is very different from, for example, Fredric Jameson's, in 'Postmodernism or the Logic of Late Capitalism'.[6] Jameson claims in this classic article that the postmodern subject cannot historicize his or her self, locate his or her self in relation to history. To us, history does not seem alive, vital. Delany claims the opposite here: that history is what is outside, in both time and space. We must know our history, because otherwise it will enslave us. The Sygn, one of the three discourses striving for hegemony in the fictional universe of *Stars*, is thus not merely analysable in a non-subsumptive, non-totalizing discourse. It *is* a non-subsumptive, non-totalizing, non-unitary discourse and the one which, if it reached hegemony, would support most possibilities for people to live without oppression.

It is not just the Sygn which has positive qualities. Delany's way of writing about the Web can be very useful for cultural theorists, trying to understand the significance of the social and political changes brought about by information technology. The Web as an information technology conglomerate is seen as essentially historical and political. The Web is not a wild, random invention. The Web, as an institution, is a displacement into an imagined universe of a theoretical construction, an historical analysis, found in our own world: the argument, made by some theorists of postmodernity, that what is significant about our late capitalist, transnational economy is the way in which information has become both a commodity and the basis of production in the service sector. Delany displaces this idea into the universe of *Stars* . The Web produces and distributes information, bringing more and more planets into its network. What is crucial here is that Delany's concept of 'politics' is a wide one, focusing on gender, race, sexuality, and class, rather than on class (or gender, or race, or sexuality) alone. As well as distributing information, the Web also disseminates an artificial language, Arachnia. This artificial language makes it possible for Delany to articulate an important political message.

Stars is about two lovers: Korga, who is a slave from Rhyonon, a world much like our own and Marq, who is from Velm, a world shared with another sentient species, the Evelm. Marq is an 'Industrial Diplomat', whose job, facilitating exchange between separate planets, brings him closer than he would like to the spiders' interests. Delany's character, Marq, thinks, on his way to a meeting with a senior Web official, a 'Black Widow', 'as the interstellar agency in charge of the general flow of information about the universe in many places, the Web is near to being torn apart by the conflict between the Sygn and the Family' (p. 87, syntax slightly rearranged). However, Marq is too close to the Web to see it clearly. He is not just close to its political interests, he quite literally speaks its language. He speaks Arachnia.

Delany's novel is in three parts. The first, dealing with Korga's story before he meets Marq, is written in the third person. The second and third parts are in the first person, narrated by Marq Dyeth. The novel, *Stars*, is thus written, for the most part, as if it were an unembellished translation of a text written in the fictional language, Arachnia, disseminated by the Web.

Arachnia does not mark gender or species difference in pronouns or in the words which would be translated, in English, by 'man' or 'woman' . The word 'woman' refers to a person of any species or gender. If arachne-speakers wish to identify someone's sex, they have to use a qualifier: a female woman, a male woman. As 'woman', in Arachnia, refers to a person of any sex or species, the pronoun one uses, in Arachnia, when refering to a person, is 'she'. The pronoun 'he' is reserved for the object of desire.

Delany's artificial language, Arachnia, spoken and disseminated by the 'spiders' who construct and maintain the network of information linking all the planets in the fictional universe described in *Stars*, is used in a construction of radical difference, rather than simply a deconstruction of identity.

This construction of radical difference is made possible by the Web, the political grouping which controls and disseminates both information and information technology in the multiplanetary economy of the imagined future space. In this way, Delany shows that the institution striving for hegemony in the fictional universe of *Stars*, the information technology Web, must be analysed in terms of both gender and class (or capital).

Even though 'he', in Arachnia, can be used by any woman, female or male, of any species, it so happens that Marq, the arachne-speaking woman who narrates most of the story is a gay, male human, attracted to male humans and male or neuter Evelm. Thus 'he', in the story, is not used to refer to females, even though 'he' in Arachnia can refer to whichever gender and species the enunciator is attracted. The only arachne-speaking voice is Marq's; Marq's narrative uses 'he', when referring to humans, with the same biological referent as in the mundane, non-SF world and with a referent that overlaps with the mundane referent when applied to aliens.

The effect of this is to deconstruct any preconceptions the reader might have of gender or species identity, creating a remarkably fluid sense of multiple difference. The text is about women, but it does not construct a fixed gender or species identity for these women. In most texts where the generic masculine is used, the writer usually shifts between a generic use of the masculine and a specific use of the masculine. Sometimes 'he' means 'a male person', sometimes 'he' means 'a person'. The effect of this, as has been frequently argued, is to universalize the male, that is, to construct the male as the subject and the female as Other. However, in *Stars*, this universal category, 'woman', remains always universal, never particular. It is very difficult, sometimes impossible, to tell, from Delany's descriptions, if this woman is female or male, human or alien. The reader is presented with a set of multiple possibilities, which remain fluid, in most cases. Only from time to time does Delany provide a detail in a description which would make more sense given one particular gender or species identity.

However, when the narrator Marq uses the pronoun 'he' the text shifts from the representation of multiple difference to the representation of identity, fixing and describing the objects of desire only as male human, male Evelm, and neuter Evelm. The effect of the shift from an universal, never particular 'she' and 'woman' to a particular, male 'he' (or, if the reference is to a member of the three-sexed Evelm species, a male or neuter 'he') is to combine the stress on and representation of an always fluid difference with a writing of identity. The identity represented in Marq's narrative is a displacement into the fictional universe of a specific gay male identity found in our world, in the recent past. It is a pre-AIDS, urban, gay male identity, constructed within a social/spatial institution which enables a multiple-partnered sexuality. Judith Butler's question 'What other local strategies for engaging the "unnatural" might lead to the denaturalization of gender as such?' is thus central for Delany's text.7 The text is about such a 'local strategy' and it succeeds brilliantly in not just denaturalizing gender but in describing and deconstructing naturalization itself.

Marq's lover, Korga, is a representation of slavery, bound in opposition to knowledge. Korga is enslaved after being subjected to a surgical procedure which deprives him of the ability to process new information, the capacity to judge, to question, and to make decisions. When he is rescued by the Web, they provide him with a prosthesis which gives him access to the kind of knowledge which is a prerequisite for gathering other knowledge, and a new facility to use and question the use of language. Delany, here, comes down firmly on the side of knowledge as liberatory, simply freeing it from (more nineteenth-century) organicist connotations. Korga, as both slave and free, is a cyborg. Liberation is not associated with either the notion of 'expression' or the notion of a 'true nature'. 'Nature' is not opposed to artifice. Instead, liberation is associated with knowledge, and knowledge is accessed by means of technology. The technologies which mediate and enable knowledge in the imagined universe of *Stars*, are implants and protheses, the use of which make the characters cyborgs, partly human, partly machine. Science and technology become part of us, rather than being opposed to us. And the technology that has become part of us, that has changed us, has made us cyborgs, can be either oppressive or liberatory. Cyborg identities can be liberatory and politically enabling, given the ways in which oppressed subjects have historically been disempowered by being associated with 'nature' in opposition to 'culture', as Donna Haraway argues in 'A Cyborg Manifesto',8 or they can just be more of the same.

The third faction, the third institution Delany represents in *Stars,* the Family, is a homophobic universalization. If the Sygn is the radical possibility for change, the Family is oppression, 'Back to Basics'.

The Thants, who have recently become politically aligned with the Family, have been invited to a formal party given by the Dyeths. The Thants signal their new allegiance by being rude to the Dyeths. They ignore their hosts, interfering with the serving of the meal . They speak to each other in a way that to persons from our world is a recognizably offensive, homophobic description of the Dyeth multisexual, multispecies collectivity, a kinship 'Stream' in which there are, in Marq's expression, 'no egg-and-sperm relations between ripples'. These characters, the Thants, are speciesist as well as homophobic. A displacement and reversal of the colonialist history in which species difference was used to construct racial ideologies is also legible in this passage. In this fictive SF universe speciesist ideology rests on racism, as well as being tied to compulsory reproductive heterosexuality, as these comments show:

> . . .reduced to animals who copulate with animals, call animals their sisters and mothers. . .
>
> . . .not as if they don't acknowledge it themselves. Our way is older, purer, human. And animal as they are and act, they know it.
>
> . . .eat and procreate, eat and—but one can't even say that. Not only the males with the females, but the males do it with males, the females do it with females, within the race, across the races—and what are we to make of neuters—as if they had not even reached the elementary stage of culture, however ignorant, where a family takes its appropriate course. (Delany, pp. 326-7, ellipses added.)

In this fictive universe the Thants' homophobia and speciesism are articulated by means of a mundane discourse of which they are themselves both support and vehicle: 'The Family'. However, Marq, the arachne-speaker, living in and constructing a space in which all species identities, gender identities, sexual identities are possible, in which all differences articulate within a discourse in which each makes sense and none makes nonsense of the others, finds the Thants' homophobia and speciesism utterly incomprehensible.

Delany's novel, *Stars In My Pockets Like Grains of Sand,* is a narrative about local spaces with local histories, local strategies for engaging the 'unnatural', told in a widely disseminated but non-universal language. In this language gender and species difference cannot be named, any subject can desire any other, the enunciation of desire is marked, but the desiring subject's identity and the identity of the object of desire is not determined. Delany's narrative and this fictional language construct only difference; they deconstruct sexual identity, gender identity, and species identity.

Notes

1. Samuel R. Delany, *Stars In My Pockets Like Grains of Sand* (New York: Bantam Books, 1984).
2. See 'The Biopolitics of Postmodern Bodies: Constitutions of Self in Immune System Discourse' in Donna Haraway, *Simians, Cyborgs and Women: The Reinvention of Nature* (New York: Routledge and Kegan Paul, 1991) 203-230, for Haraway's most detailed discussion of information science and its relation to both biological science, the human bodies/embodied humans who are the objects and subjects of the biological and medical sciences, and contemporary North American postmodern political, economic, and cultural institutions, historical processes, and subjects.
3. See Clifford Geertz, *Local Knowledge* (New York: Basic Books, 1983).

4. See David Harvey, *The Condition of Postmodernity* (Oxford: Blackwell, 1989).

5. See Mike Davis, *Prisoners of the American Dream* (London: Verso, 1986) and *City of Quartz* (New York, Vintage Books, 1990).

6. Fredric Jameson, 'Postmodernism or the Logic of Late Capitalism', *New Left Review*, July/August 1984, 53-94.

7. Judith Butler's *Gender Trouble* (London: Routledge and Kegan Paul, 1990) is a radical, constructivist account of gender. She argues that all gender formations are constructed through performance, but that one binary set of gender formations, linked to a prescriptive hetero-sexuality, is made to appear the norm. Only one kind of masculinity and one kind of femininity is made to appear 'natural' and all other genderings are made to seem 'unnatural' and even incomprehensible. However, there are plenty of other genderings, plenty of ways in which people challenge the norms of their society, plenty of local spaces, gay or lesbian communities for example, which mount a challenge to the normativizing tendencies of contemporary society.

8. Donna Haraway, 'A Cyborg Manifesto', in Haraway, *Simians, Cyborgs and Women*, 149-181.

Interactive Fiction and Narrative Space

Andrew Gibson
Department of English
Royal Holloway, University of London

The chief concern of this essay is the relationship between narrative theory and interactive fiction (IF).[1] Potentially, at least, this relationship is a fertile field of enquiry for two reasons. On the one hand, interactive fiction poses some radical challenges to the theoretical models and modes of thought that are currently dominant in narrative theory. On the other, a more sophisticated grasp of narrative theory—its history, current state and most debated issues—would arguably radicalize the programmers' and enthusiasts' sense of the possibilities made available by the new medium. In practice, however, so far as I know, little or nothing of interest has emerged to connect these two fields of activity. The reasons for this are partly obvious: narrative theory has emerged out of disciplines like English Studies, that have seldom been overly inclined to keep pace with the progress of the new technology, save as it offers a new tool for the old endeavours. From the perspective of such disciplines—except, perhaps, in hypertext form—IF is likely to seem a more or less trivial and indeed conservative kind of popular culture. After all, those recently most enthusiastically engaged in designing computerized forms of narrative have included Clive Barker and Terry Pratchett. Sexism, violence, even soft porn: all are distinctive features of certain computer games. The conservatism of the genre can be overstated: Cyro's *KGB* turns the player into a KGB agent involved in a conspiracy, and *Spring Break* is arguably a parody of sexual stereotypes in which the weakling vanquishes the muscle men. But the reactionary label can nonetheless easily be made to stick. It is interesting to note, too, how often those who write about adventure games refer back to certain kinds of literature—Tolkien, C. S. Lewis—and, sometimes nervously, to the opinions of English professors. Yet, at the same time, the theorizations of IF that have been emerging from the practitioners and aficionados have been largely oblivious to the most significant trends and important issues in contemporary narrative theory (and critical theory). They have tended to return to what, in terms of the history of narrative theory, are classical sources (Aristotle, Propp) or to rely on extraneous authorities (Joseph Campbell).[2] They have seldom looked across the way to developments in narrative theory that might be thought of as having emerged concurrently with the development and progress of IF. This is understandable enough, in the case of a fledgeling genre casting around for its first theoretical foundations. But it nonetheless misses out on what are surely interesting possibilities for productive exchange and dialogue. It is precisely such a dialogue that I am trying to begin in this essay.

Current narrative theory or narratology is a quite distinctive phenomenon. It emerged in the late Sixties and early Seventies out of French structuralism. But where the deconstructive turn of the late Seventies and early Eighties brought an end to structuralism, narratology survived deconstruction and has continued to flourish; not so much in Britain, perhaps, where it had only a limited purchase from the start, but in Europe, Israel, Japan, and, most of all, the USA. One of the reasons for the survival of narratology through the Eighties and on into the Nineties was the emergence of a form of revisionism in narrative theory as exemplified in the work of a range of figures like Peter Brooks, Ross Chambers, Karl Kroeber, and James Phelan, and even, to some extent, in feminist narrative theory, as in the work of Susan Lanser and Robyn Warhol.3 Narrative theory in the Eighties was dominated by revisionism. Revisionist narrative theory gave itself out as in one respect or another a move beyond structuralism. But it also deployed its critique of structuralism to re-establish certain theoretical premises and unexamined assumptions that had consistently underpinned the humanist traditions that had been dominant in thought about narrative prior to structuralism. In other words, narrative theory over the past decade has been caught in, even cultivated, a theoretical double-bind whereby it announces itself as both post- and pre-structuralist. Recently, however, there have been signs of further changes and transformations. In two recent books, for example, both Didier Coste and Marcel Cornis-Pope have been arguing the need for a kind of deconstructive operation on narratology itself.4 The issue that is now increasingly haunting narratology is precisely this: how much longer can the latter continue to protect itself from all the various and diverse forms of deconstructive, postmodern, or other critical theory now available? I have tried to address this issue myself in *Towards a Postmodern Theory of Narrative*, which draws precisely on a wide range of contemporary critical theory in order to deconstruct the narratological system, and to explore the possibility of developing new modes of theorizing narrative, partly in relation to emergent forms of narrative like IF.5

One central plank in the case against narratology as I develop it in in my book is that narratology has insistently been haunted by a form of what Derrida calls 'geometrics'. Strictly speaking, traditionally, narratology has repeatedly projected its object or objects in terms of two kinds of space. On the one hand, there is the space limned by mimesis, construed as real space, the singular, uniform space of the real world. On the other hand, there is textual or, better, structural space, the space of the model, decidable form. In this second dimension, the narratological imaginary has been haunted by a dream of Euclidean geometry. It has been pervaded by a 'geometrics', in the sense in which Derrida uses that term in his essay 'Force and Signification'. For a structuralist, says Derrida, specifically, in this instance, Jean Rousset:

the notion of structure refers only to space, geometric or morphological space, the order of forms and sites. Structure is first the structure of an organic or artificial work, the internal unity of an assemblage, a *construction*; a work that is governed by a unifying principle, the *architecture* that is built and made visible in a location.[6]

'This geometry is only metaphorical, it will be said', writes Derrida:

Certainly. But metaphor is never innocent. It orients research and fixes results. When the spatial model is hit upon, when it functions, critical reflection rests within it. In fact, and even if criticism does not admit this to be so.[7]

It is precisely the geometric 'spatial model' within which narratology has 'rested'. It was precisely this kind of spatial model, for example, that underlay the most important models of 'deep' narrative structure as developed by Lévi-Strauss and Greimas.[8] It was the same 'geometrics' that underlay narratological story models from Propp to Bremond.[9] It was equally evident in that classic of narrative theory, Roland Barthes's *S\Z*. Everywhere in narrative theory, traditional, humanist, structuralist, and revisionist, the text, texts, or textual system have been reduced to the geometric diagram, petrified within a geometric system of description. This is everywhere evident in the best, best known, and most comprehensive descriptions of what is deemed to be the 'narrative system': Mieke Bal's, Slomith Rimmon-Kenan's, and, most famously, Gérard Genette's.[10] Indeed, Genette's account of how it is possible to dream that Proust's *Recherche du temps perdu* is illustrative of the narrative system as a whole takes place precisely in the terms which, for Derrida, leave Rousset's 'geometrics' open to interrogation:

each of [the *Recherche*'s] analysable features lends itself to some connection, comparison, or putting into perspective. Like every work, like every organism, the *Recherche* is made up of elements that are universal, or at least transindividual, which it assembles into a specific synthesis, into a particular totality.[11]

This 'totality' is a geometric 'grid'. The 'grid' of Proust's *Recherche*—and of the narrative system—which Genette produces is not, he asserts, 'an instrument of incarceration, of bringing to heel, or of pruning that in fact castrates: it is a procedure of discovery, and a way of describing'.[12] The contrary seems to me to be the case: everywhere in Genettian theory— narrative theory—the text is neatly segmented, symmetrically mapped, closed in and closed down by the geometric mode of description. Nor did this geometrization of the narrative text suddenly occur with structuralism, as part of its break with older, humanistic methodologies. Rather, there was no such decisive break. In this respect, as I argue in *Towards a Postmodern Theory of Narrative*, structuralist methodology appears as actually a kind of culmination or fulfilment of lines of thought already apparent in more classical approaches to narrative from Henry James through neo-Aristoteleanism to Wayne Booth. Yet—to paraphrase and add to

Derrida—narratological geometrization takes place only at the price of a diminution of narrative energy and ardour, narrative as force and as event. In more Heideggerian terms—which I take to be partly Derrida's—narratology represents the triumph of techno-science over the poetic, obscuring what Heidegger in 'The Origin of the Work of Art' calls the 'letting happen' of the truth and the event, what cannot be 'proved and derived from what went before'.[13]

It is evidently odd, however, to invoke the Heideggerian conception of techno-science in a volume like this. After all, for Heidegger, the technological *Gestell* is the very accomplishment of nihilism. Yet, as the homogenizing descriptions of 'techno-science' that emerge out of Heidegger's romantic negativity are obviously problematic, so, too, there are different post-Heideggerian ways of engaging with technology and technological culture. This is the case with interactive fiction. It is easy enough to read IF, its enthusiasts, and their accounts of IF, as quite obsessively 'geometric'. As I said earlier, the practitioners are sometimes noticeably conservative. Indeed, their conception of narrative can easily be made to look positively banal. Michael Graves, for example, games producer for Interplay, can be found emphasizing 'the mission to entertain': better plots, better characterization, an enhanced impression of 'reality', 'just as though you're reading a book'.[14] More importantly, the more sophisticated enthusiasts tend to be classical in their tastes in narrative theory. Aristotle, for example, is understood as a kind of arch-grammarian of narrative—by Brenda Laurel, for instance—precisely in the sense in which Todorov aspired to be such a grammarian: as distinguishing a limited set of narrative units, to be combined into a structure with a geometrical clarity, regularity, symmetry, and sense of proportion.[15] Propp is cited as a kind of proto-structuralist whose description of narrative elements allows for the construction of new, computer-based narratives as well-proportioned buildings, like Henry James's storied house of fiction. The geometric diagram recurs in accounts of IF as it does in narratology. One of the most blatant examples would be Christa Hansen's argument for establishing 'orthogonal emotional variables' in programming.[16] Graves writes of the model of the narrative world, for example, as a list of containers: 'cities contain houses, houses contain rooms, rooms contain things, things contain other things.'[17] The metaphor of 'container representation', as Graves calls it, is precisely analogous to those images of hierarchies of levels, boxes within boxes, *mises en abyme*, embeddings and the like that have been so beloved of narratologists. Indeed, it is not hard to see how appropriate such metaphors might seem to be to IF. So, too, Graves's and others' metaphors of 'frames' and 'stacks' have their exact equivalent in narratological geometrics. It is even true that, far from there merely being analogies between the geometrics of narratology and IF theory, artificial intelligence (AI), at least, has recently been providing a formidable support for narratological geometrics itself. One peculiarly striking example of this would be Marie-Laure Ryan's *Possible Worlds: Artificial Intelligence and Narrative Theory*, where models derived from AI actually contribute to a massive consolidation and extension of narratological geometrics, and one of the fiercest exclusions yet from the field of narratology of forms of narrative that are obviously not reducible to the geometric diagram.[18]

Yet neither IF itself nor what the enthusiasts have been saying about it can simply be reduced to an establishment or confirmation of geometrical models. Greg Costikyan, for example, has recently argued that interactive fictions are not stories and are inherently non-linear.[19] Certain distinctions might clearly be in order here. Some games are more linear than others: *Kyrandia I*, for example, as opposed to *Hand of Fate*. The much-praised and highly rated recent LucasArts adventures (*Day of the Tentacle, Secret of Monkey Island 2, Indiana Jones and the Fate of Atlantis*) are intrinsically less linear, by and large, than the cruder Sierra games like the *Space Quest* adventures. Interestingly, there are currently lively arguments among the enthusiasts about how complex the 'interfaces' (moments when decisions are made) should actually be. Should the player be able to engage in pointless conversations, for example, or actions that have no goal? At all events, it is clear that, whilst there may be a linear default path through IF—a clear, sequential plot—that plot cannot be thought of as in any respect the essence of the narrative in question. Rather, it exists as simply one among myriad possibilities, a kind of Platonic ideal of the narrative line which is never that of the actual narrative as it emerges or fails to emerge under the user's control. Narrative or the experience of narrative— for with IF, narrative and the experience of narrative become properly inseparable—involve a species of what Serres calls *errance*, or wandering, what the producers of IF call *browsing* in narrative environments, exploring a variety of different avenues leading in different directions, encountering frustrations and blocks to forward progress. As Costikyan suggests, then, the concepts appropriate to traditional narrative are finally inappropriate to interactive fiction, precisely because the narrative line has vanished, disintegrated, become merely one of a number of operable logics. But if the narrative line has gone then so, too, has the geometry of narrative space beloved of narrative theory. For the narrative line is the very foundation of that geometry.

It is surely clear, then, that models other than the standard geometrical ones are required for interactive fiction. For all their intermittent resorts to geometrics, the programmers and theorists of IF have also themselves been conceiving of IF in very different terms. Syd Mead of CyberDreams— someone, significantly, with design credits for Ridley Scott's *Blade Runner*—contrasts IF with film: in film, you 'talk' to the viewer's 'mental library', and 'you need to be rational so as not to interrupt the story'. The design for an adventure game, on the other hand, is a 'hypothetical setting' and 'you don't need logical rules'.[20] More importantly, the theorists have also been producing some very different models. David Graves writes of 'decision trees', for instance.[21] Phil Goetz introduces the concept of the 'maze of links'.[22] Goetz draws parallels between IF and Cortazar's *Hopscotch*, precisely the kind of narrative text that Ryan's narrative theory would rule out of court. Goetz also compares IF with Borges's work, as others have, particularly 'The Garden of Forking Paths'. Costikyan suggests a parallel with Cage, where 'the designer provides the theme, the players the music'.[23] In *Hamlet on the Holodeck, or Towards an Aesthetics of Cyberspace*, Janet H. Murray writes of a model which she sees as 'part of the postmodern mythos', that of the labyrinth.[24] Suggestive as all of these ideas are, none of them seems to me quite to come to terms with one particular feature of IF. IF puts the user in the place of the creator in one very specific way: it makes him or her choose from among a set of radiating possibilities in a manner hardly ever available to the reader of a novel. In other words, the shadow of the excluded possibility becomes part of the narrative itself. In interactive narrative, the possible always shadows the actual, as a kind of virtual space. This is perhaps most startlingly evident in the new adventures coming out of Revolution Software, such as *Lure of the Temptress* and *Beneath a Steel Sky*. Revolution Software have developed an innovative system called Virtual Theatre in which all characters and objects continue to move about the game whether they are on-screen or not, turning up after the initial encounter in modified forms and different locations. Indeed, it is even possible to watch characters carrying on their actions in 'other worlds', as it were. The user 'peeps in' through observation windows on what the present narrative situation is excluding. In fact, IF therefore effectively de-realizes narrative, in containing within itself and making us immediately aware of a range of narrative alternatives which might equally become or have become the narrative itself. Noel Williams would seek to deny that this is the case with adventure games:

> ... existing game structures are more limited than the kind of writing normally thought of under the IF umbrella. It is more limited because it is essentially story-telling, is based on limiting the reader's choices to a relatively narrow set of simple actions and has clearly defined goals, pathways and win/lose situations.[25]

Hypertext writing, on the other hand, 'looks to create a rich imaginative experience, like that of a conventional novel, yet through unconventional means'.[26] But it is surely the case that, in adventure games, too, narrative can no longer be imagined as constrained by certain steely determinations, however much the possibilities are arranged and contained by the programmers. Rather, the user must experience narrative itself as the simplification it always was and can only ever be; which is, at the same time, to experience the *eventuality* of narrative, narrative as emergence.

The geometric model asserts that the space of narrative is uniform and homogeneous, a single and universally valid space. The creators of IF, by contrast, seem increasingly to be delighting in creating multiple and (often radically) heterogeneous spaces. In the first instance, this is true at the simplest of levels, in the creation of multiple worlds. 'A lot of work is put into dealing with revealing a story in which the pacing is different with every player'.[27] Thus Eddie Dombrower, executive producer on Activision's *Return to Zork*. So, too, in *Ultima Underworld 2*, for instance, the user moves between eight separate worlds. The multiple spaces may be designated as time-zones, as in the case of the three separate 'worlds' in *Day of the Tentacle*; though Coktel Vision in France seem to have made this their speciality, as with *Inca*, or *Lost in Time*, where the narrative can be shifted between present-day Brittany, a Caribbean island in 1840, and 2092 AD. Equally, there are the little pleasurable or recreational spaces that are incidental to the main narrative business, as with some of the soft porn insets in certain Japanese *anime*. In *Cobra Mission*, for example, it is possible to take time off from irksome puzzle-solving and spy through a telescope on a group of scantily-clad girls. One variant on this kind of incidental space would be the game within the game, as in *Day of the Tentacle*, in which it is possible to play LucasArts's original game, *Maniac Mansion*, instead of playing *Day of the Tentacle* itself. Yet another version of heterogenous space would be the anachronistic *mélange*, as in the case of the mediaeval wizard's mud hut, complete with fridge, in *Simon the Sorcerer*, or the troubadour in *Legend* who sings Annie Lennox songs whenever the enemy annoys him. But all these examples are merely figures for a more important point: the way in which, in IF, *any specific space* is also a heterogeneous space, a space of actualization out of potentials, of a multiplicity of possible constructions. The single character in *Shadowcaster* is able to go through a range of transformations, each of his shapes having a different set of powers and limitations, a different perspective on its surroundings, a different sense of the dimensions and angles of the space observed. The experts call this 'morphing'. It is symptomatic of something written much more largely into IF: in *Ultima Underworld*, the user's actions at one stage of the narrative will determine what he or she encounters at another stage. In *Dungeon Hack*, the mazes and their contents are randomly generated at each new stage. In *Dark Seed*, not only are there two worlds, but any action the user performs in one has repercussions in the other, even though the latter is off-screen. Actuality impacts upon a virtuality and thus upon what will later become narrative actuality itself. Multiple space is also a conditional or modifiable space. Most strikingly of all, perhaps, in *Indiana Jones and the Fate of Atlantis*, there are three possible routes through the narrative material: the Fist Path, where Indiana Jones must fight; the Wits Path, on which he must think; and the Team Path, on which he joins forces with Sophia. Each path modifies the narrative situations accordingly. There is thus no fixed or single narrative space in this adventure. There is only a set of potentials which can be activated in different ways, where each activation is an event.

In the end, then, the appropriate figure for IF is arguably not the decision tree, exactly, nor the maze of links or the labyrinth, but the *parcours*, in the sense and the context which Michel Serres provides for that term. Serres has long been rejecting the geometric metaphor and elaborating a thought that works rather in terms of striated, variegated, or heterogenous space, sometimes specifically in relation to narrative. In particular, in an essay called 'Discours et Parcours' in *La Distribution*, Serres substitutes the notion of narrative *parcours* for that of narrative discourse (*discours*).[28] The narrative *parcours* is a movement through multiple spaces, an *errance*, to use that term again. It is not simply a variant on the old theme of narrative as quest or journey. It rather involves a theory of narrative that breaks radically with the unitary spaces both of representation and of narratology. It suggests that narrative continually connects up incommensurable spaces, spaces that are rigorously defined in their own right. Take Zola, for instance, on whom Serres has written at length.[29] The novels of the Rougon-Macquart series set in motion a number of different systems of circulation that are irreducible to one another. In *L'Assommoir*:

> la Gervaise ... est boiteuse. Voici la figure de la tare héréditaire, le mot tare signifiant d'abord écart à l'équilibre. Mais, d'autre part, tombé du toit, son mari, couvreur, va boiter comme elle. Gervaise est tombée: aux basses classes, au bidonville de la Goutte d'or. Elle est l'amie du forgeron, la Gueule d'or; elle est la mère de Nana, la Mouche d'or qui débute dans la carrière en jouant la blonde Vénus dans un théâtre parisien. Voici qu'en suivant à la trace la légende dorée, vous reconstituez toute l'affaire de Vulcain, dont l'antre, justement, est reconstitué sur les tréteaux. Gervaise boite par la tare, elle se déhanche par la chute. Le savoir fait, d'un coup, silence, la mythologie parle ... une fois filtrés les contenus dit scientifiques, il reste un résidu où un jeu de circulation organise des reprises mythiques.[30]

What is at issue here is a principle of topological heterogeneity which makes of Zola's novel a kind of knitting together of distinct spaces (in this instance, the mythological and the contemporary scientific). The space of the *parcours* is never a singular space. The *parcours* is rather to be traced between varied spaces without common borders, through junctions achieved with difficulty where communication has been cut. In all such cases, says Serres:

> il y va de connexion et non-connexion, il y va de l'espace, il y va du parcours. Et donc l'essentiel n'est plus cette figure, ce symbole ou cet artefact, l'invariant formel est quelque chose comme un transport, une errance, un voyage àtravers des variétés spatiales séparées. La circumnavigation d'Ulysse ou de Gilgamesh et la topologie.[31]

Ulysses, Gilgamesh—and Oedipus, too: again and again, in the most ancient myths, narrative becomes 'la mise en place de séparations entre espaces et leur liaison difficile'.[32] Narrative, here, is a complex weave, a network of connections, a graph:

> le parcours oedipien franchit les accidents spatiaux, bifurcations, catastrophes et boucles. Le discours oedipien est indentiquement ce parcours. Il pose ... des carrefours entre des variétés qui ne sont pas à bord commun. Ce qui suppose qu'avant lui, c'est-à-dire avant le discours, il existait une multiplicité d'espaces sans rapport, le chaos.[33]

So, too, in the case of the story of Ulysses, *discours* is *parcours*, a composition of numerous spatial categories which cannot be reduced to homogeneity or uniformity; as though the aim and impulse of narrative itself were connection, above all.

This, for Serres, is precisely the politics of narrative. There is a sense in which, for Serres—unlike, say, Bakhtin—narrative is a positively utopian form. It throws bridges across divides, forms links between irreducible disparates, establishes relations between 'les niches écologiques séparées, défendues bec et ongles'.[34] One way of putting the point would be to suggest that, for Serres, the narrative principle is an erotic principle, or, at least, that it works ceaselessly to reduce the distance between antagonistic elements without at the same time reducing one to the terms of the other or denying their incommensurability. In the case of Serres's account of the Oedipus myth, narrative finds a certain kind of equivalent in the figure of the Sphinx, itself a hybrid form in which elements of disparate beings have been stitched together. The Sphinx is the embodiment of the principle of bifurcation or the crossroads evident everywhere in the Oedipus myth. Hence the fact, says Serres, that we might usefully conceive of narrative space as ultimately chimerical. But a still more significant figure, for Serres, is that of Penelope, the weaver, 'la reine qui tisse et détisse, le féminin premier':

> Voici que se lève l'image du tisserand. De lier, de nouer, de pratiquer des ponts, des chemins, des puits ou des relais, parmi des espaces radicalement différents. De dire ce qui se passe entre eux. D'inter-dire. La catégorie *entre*, fondamentale en topologie et ici.[35]

We might wish to consider the appropriateness of the image of the 'tisserand' or 'weaver' for narrative precisely as it is opposed to the Euclidean space hitherto so unremittingly promoted by narratology. Indeed, we might wonder whether it is not Euclidean space that is most at odds with narrative as a principle of 'connection'. For in Euclidean space, at least as it is endemic to narrative theory, displacement would always appear to be possible without a change of state. The *parcours* thus becomes merely the movement of a self-identical being through a homogeneous exteriority. Euclidean space, says Serres, represses a 'topologie sauvage' that we hardly know how to begin to get back to, even today. It represses that 'topologie' precisely in the name of the universal.

If the *parcours* is the mode of the most ancient narratives, I would finally also suggest that postmodernity is increasingly returning to and linking up with that most ancient mode. In this respect, IF has claims to being the postmodern mode of narrative *par excellence*. IF is a major instance of a postmodernity which is increasingly producing narrative as a fluid relation of multiple spaces, thereby opening up the possibility of reading other narratives in similar terms. In various aspects of their lives, from channel-surfing to the Internet, to drugs, casual travel, and separated parents, a younger generation is becoming more and more attuned to a world that, for them, increasingly exists as such a 'multiplicity'. The hermeneutic obsessions of, say, literature departments are bound to look more and more creaky and arthritic in comparison. At all events, whilst I have raised one or two doubts about the ultimate adequacy of their models, Murray, Goetz, and Costikyan are all surely right to suggest that the interesting connections are between IF and the postmodern avant-garde, rather than IF and Aristotle, Propp, or the classic realist text. For in IF as in Cortazar or Robbe-Grillet, for example, narrative again reveals itself as *parcours*, and with a quite startling clarity. Narrative, then, is *parcours*, and it is only hermeneutics and naratological geometrics that keep us from that fact: geometrics, in that it freezes heterogeneity, possibility, and difference into homogeneity and uniformity; hermeneutics, in that it relentlessly displaces questions of heterogeneity into questions of mere meaning.

Notes

1. The term 'interactive fiction' has been used and understood in various ways. Noel Williams applies it only to hypertext fiction as opposed to adventure games. See Williams, 'Computers and Writing', in Christopher S. Butler (ed.), *Computers and Written Texts* (Oxford: Blackwell, 1992), 247-66. Phil Goetz also argues that 'interactive fiction does not equal adventures'. See Goetz, 'Interactive Fiction and Computers', *Inter*Action*, 1 (September 1994), 98-115. For David Graves, on the other hand, 'interactive fiction' is any form of fiction which allows the reader 'some degree of interaction with the story', including pick-a-path books, for instance. See Graves, 'Frequently Asked Questions on rec. arts. int-fiction', (August 1993, dag@cup.hp.com). A definition even larger than Graves's is adopted by the journal *Inter*Action* (now *Interactive Fantasy*), which claims to concern itself with all 'the many forms of interactive fiction', from RPGs (role-playing games) to boardgame systems, live role-playing, and re-enactment games. My own use of the term refers only to computerized forms of interactive narrative, but includes the various forms of so-called 'adventure games' along with hypertext fiction. In the discussion that follows, my examples are primarily 'adventure games'.

2. See for instance Graves, 'Questions'; Brenda Laurel, 'Towards the Design of a Computer-Based Interactive Fantasy System', Ph.D thesis (Ohio State University, 1986); Andrew Rilstone, Greg Stafford, and James Wallis, 'Sigmund Freud and Joseph Campbell', *Interactive Fantasy*, 2 (December 1994), 43-56; and James Wallis, review of *Simulation and Gaming*, Vol. 25, no. 2, in *Interactive Fantasy*, 2, 155-56.

3. See Peter Brooks, *Reading for the Plot: Design and Intention in Narrative* (New York: Vintage, 1984); Ross Chambers, *Story and Situation: Narrative Seduction and the Power of Fiction* (Minneapolis: University of Minnesota Press, 1984) and *Room for Maneuver: Reading Oppositional Narrative* (Chicago: University of Chicago Press, 1991); Karl Kroeber, *Retelling/Rereading: The Fate of Storytelling in Modern Times* (New Brunswick, NJ: Rutgers University Press, 1990); James Phelan, *Reading People, Reading Plots: Character, Progression and the Interpretation of Narrative* (Chicago: University of Chicago Press, 1989); Susan Sniader Lanser, 'Towards a Feminist Narratology', in Robyn R. Warhol, and Diane Price Herndl, (eds.), *Feminisms: An Anthology of Literary Theory and Criticism* (New Brunswick: Rutgers University Press, 1991), 610-29; and *Fictions of Authority: Women Writers and the Narrative Voice* (Ithaca and London: Cornell University Press, 1992); and Robyn Warhol, *Gendered Interventions: Narrative Discourse in the Victorian Novel* (New Brunswick and London: Rutgers University Press, 1989).

4. See Marcel Cornis-Pope, *Hermeneutic Desire and Critical Rewriting: Narrative Interpretation in the Wake of Poststructuralism* (London: Macmillan, 1992); and Didier Coste, *Narrative as Communication*, with a foreword by Wlad Godzich, (Minneapolis: University of Minnesota Press, 1989).

5. See *Towards a Postmodern Theory of Narrative* (Hemel Hempstead: Harvester Wheatsheaf, forthcoming in 1996).

6. Jacques Derrida, 'Force and Signification', in *Writing and Difference*, tr. with an introduction and additional notes by Alan Bass, (London: Routledge and Kegan Paul, 1978), 3-30, 15.

7. Ibid. 17.

8. See Claude Lévi-Strauss, *Structural Anthropology* (New York: Doubleday Anchor Books, 1968); Algirdas Julien Greimas, *Sémantique Structurale: Recherche de Méthode* (Paris: Larousse, 1966) and *Du Sens* (Paris: Éditions du Seuil, 1970).

9. See Vladimir Propp, *Morphology of the Folk Tale*, tr. Laurence Scott (Austin: University of Texas Press, 1968); and Claude Bremond, *Logique du Récit* (Paris: Seuil, 1973)

10. See Mieke Bal, *Narratology: Introduction to the Theory of Narrative*, tr. Christine Van Boheemen (London: University of Toronto Press, 1985); Slomith Rimmon-Kenan, *Narrative Fiction: Contemporary Poetics* (London: Methuen, 1983); and Gérard Genette, *Narrative Discourse*, tr.

Jane E. Lewin, with a foreword by Jonathan Culler (Oxford: Blackwell, 1980).

11. Genette, *Narrative Discourse*, 23.

12. Ibid. 265.

13. Martin Heidegger, 'The Origin of the Work of Art', in *Poetry, Language, Thought*, tr. with an introduction by Albert Hofstadter (London: Harper and Row, 1971), 15-89, 36.

14. See Sharon Greaves, 'Hollywood Ate my Video Game', *PC Action*, 2 (Christmas, 1993), 14-15.

15. For Laurel, see note 2. For Todorov on the 'grammar' of narrative, see his *Grammaire du Décaméron* (Paris: Mouton, 1969).

16. Quoted in David Graves 'Bringing Characters to Life', in *Journal of Computer Game Design*, 2.2 (December 1988), 10-11.

17. David Graves, 'Second Generation Adventure Games', in *Journal of Computer Game Design*, 1.2 (August 1987), 4-7.

18. Marie-Laure Ryan, *Possible Worlds, Artificial Intelligence and Narrative Theory* (Bloomington and London: Indiana University Press, 1991). For further confirmation of what I take to be the conservatism of Ryan's position, see her 'The Modes of Narrativity and their Visual Metaphors' in Jacqueline Berben-Masi (ed.), *Narrative in Nice, Style*, 26.3 (Fall 1992), 368-87.

19. Greg Costikyan, 'I Have No Words and I Must Design', *Interactive Fantasy*, 1.2 (December 1994), 22-39, 23.

20. Sharon Greaves, 'Hollywood Ate my Video Game', 15.

21. David Graves, 'Plot Automation,' *Journal of Computer Game Design*, 5.1 (October 1991), 10-12.

22. Phil Goetz, 'Interactive Fiction and Computers', 100.

23. Greg Costikyan, 'I Have No Words and I Must Design', 24.

24. Janet H. Murray, *Hamlet on the Holodeck, or Towards an Aesthetics of Cyberspace* (forthcoming).

25. Williams, 'Computers and Writing', 262. (See note 1.)

26. Ibid. 262

27. See Sharon Greaves, 'Hollywood Ate my Video Game', 16.

28. Michel Serres, 'Discours et Parcours', in *Hermès IV: la distribution* (Paris: Éditions de Minuit, 1977), 197-210. All translations mine. Serres's work is likely to be less familiar to English readers than that of other recent French thinkers because comparatively little of it is as yet available in translation. An extensive account of various aspects of his thought may be found in my *Towards a Postmodern Theory of Narrative*.

29. See Serres, *Feux et signaux de brume: Zola* (Paris: Grasset, 1975).

30. 'Gervaise ... is lame. There we have the figure of the hereditary defect, the word 'defect' first signifying a divergence from equilibrium. But on the other hand, once he has fallen from the roof, her husband, the roofer, will limp like her. Gervaise herself has fallen: into the lower

classes, the shanty town of the Goutte d'Or [Drop of Gold]. She is a friend of the blacksmith's, of the 'golden mouth'. She is the mother of Nana, the gilded fly who begins her career by playing a blonde Venus in a Parisian theatre. There, in following the trace of the legend of gold, you reconstitute the whole affair of Vulcan, whose cave has itself been reconstituted on the stage. Gervaise limps because of her defect, and dislocates her hip in her fall. Knowledge is suddenly silent, mythology speaks ... once the so-called scientific contents are filtered off, there remains a residue in which a game of circulation organizes certain mythic repetitions.' Serres, 'Discours et Parcours', 198-99.

31. 'It is a question of connection and non-connection, of space, of the *parcours*. Thus what is essential is no longer this or that figure, symbol, or artefact. The formal invariant is something like a transport or wandering, a voyage across a variety of separate spaces. The circumnavigation of a Ulysses or a Gilgamesh, and topology'. Serres, 'Discours et Parcours', 200.

32. '... the placing of separations between spaces and the difficult activity of connecting them'. Serres, 'Discours et Parcours', 204. See 204-5 for Serres's account of the Oedipus story as a narrative of 'multiple spaces'.

33. 'The *parcours* of Oedipus makes its way through spatial accidents, bifurcations, catastrophes, loops. Oedipean discourse is identical with this *parcours*. It places ... crossroads between varieties that have no common border. This necessarily supposes that before it, that is to say, before discourse, there was only chaos, a multiplicity of spaces with no relation to one another'. Serres, 'Discours et Parcours', 206.

34. '... separate ecological niches, defended tooth and claw'. Serres, 'Discours et Parcours', 208.

35. 'Here the image of the weaver comes to mind. Of tying, knotting, using bridges, roads, wells, relays, among radically different spaces. Saying what happens between them. Inter-dicting. The category 'between', fundamental in topology and here'. Serres, 'Discours et Parcours', 207, 202.

Sexualized Bodies in Cyberspace

Nina Wakeford
Department of Sociological Studies
University of Sheffield

A virtual fieldwork anecdote. In 1990 I was drawn out of the library and into cyberspace by 'Sappho', an e-mail discussion list maintained in Boston, USA.[1] After several days of watching the list for clues about how to construct my first 'appearance', I typed an introduction: I was a graduate student from England, studying sociology, and new to the list and this kind of electronic communication. Some hours later two replies had been posted to the whole list . The first said 'Hi there cute English babe!', to which someone else had replied 'Hands off, I saw her first!'. It was a shock. I had never been approached like this anywhere else. Being fought over by unknown women felt unreal, yet thrilling. In the following days I received a series of public and private posts asking for more details about myself. The most common question was 'What do you *look* like?'. How I responded to such interrogation formed an integral part of my first experiences of creating and maintaining an identity in cyberspace.

The study of bodies is in vogue, and judging by recent popular media attention, so is cyberspace. This paper investigates what happens when the two performances of bodies and cyberspace intersect. As such, it is a preliminary intervention in the emerging sociology of cyberspace, computer-mediated communication, and information technologies. My focus is the body in cyberspace, and specifically a convention which I refer to as textual bodywork, which occurs on Sappho.

Bodies and cyberspace have leaky boundaries, and I find it helpful to think of both as strategic performances, particularly in relation to their textual creation in certain modes of computer-mediated communication. I will attempt to engage with debates about both bodies and cyberspace before I show how they intersect in the practice of textual bodywork on Sappho. My own search for bodies has been influenced by the work of Donna Haraway and of Sandy Stone, and the ways in which they rethink the boundaries between nature, technology, and society.[2] Although bodies are conventionally cast as being grounded in the physical/biological/ natural, as both Stone and Haraway stress in their work, treating nature, technology, and society as separate analytical categories may be unreliable. The construction of a physical, biological, and natural body may be nothing more than a device which ensures a boundary with technology. One of the many boundary transgressions which cross-cuts nature, technology, and society is Haraway's well known formulation that 'I would rather be a cyborg than a goddess'.[3] For Haraway, the cyborg condition, part-human part-machine, is not only a way of characterizing a condition of contemporary experience but also a strategic position for an anti-racist

93

feminist theory. My interest in textual bodywork stems from the attempt to investigate how a theoretical formulation of the cyborg can help to understand the lived realities of users of computer-mediated communication within the more unstable category of cyberspace.

The struggle about the definition of cyberspace has yet to reach any clear consensus. The characterization of this space as a 'consensual hallucination' by William Gibson in his novel *Neuromancer* (1984) is cited by many authors as a significant historical moment in the evolution of a definition, yet to ground a concept solely in terms of science fiction risks distracting our attention from the activities of those who participate in something which they construct as cyberspace as part of their non-fictional daily practices.[4] Michael Benedikt potentially adds to the confusion in his introduction to the collection *Cyberspace: First Steps* by beginning ten separate paragraphs 'Cyberspace:' followed by explanations and commentaries which vary in content and tone. In this way he resists any attempt to restrict the word to a unitary definition.[5] Amongst other things, cyberspace is:'A word from the pen of William Gibson. . .A new universe. . .A common mental geography. . .The realm of pure information.'[6] Although initially confusing, such resistance to a single definition side-steps the problem of enforcing rigid boundaries of what is and what is not cyberspace. Boundary formation is in itself an exclusionary practice which is particularly unhelpful in an area which is in constant flux. If the desire for a unitary definition itself represents a consensual hallucination on the part of those attempting to theorize about it (and this might indeed be the case) then the exclusionary practice which attempts to place boundaries around 'true' cyberspace also reproduces a discourse which hints at a gate-keeping function: who claims to create or participate in the 'real' thing.

If it is difficult to articulate theoretically the word cyberspace, it is perhaps easier to track down how its performance is being constructed currently by popular culture. Among the sudden outpouring of media representations, cyberpunk and hacker culture are still presented as part of the subcultural heritage of cyberspace. At the same time a wider construction is reframing cyberspace as a commodity sustained by mainstream cultural industries. Promises of something called cyberspace are flaunted to tempt a moneyed audience to buy software, hardware, and a crop of new magazines. Few publications resist the urge to present cyberspace in combinations of primary/neon colours and black, and magazines such as *.net* and *Internet Today* seem to be trying to forge a space between unreconstructed computer magazines (e.g. *PC Weekly*) and lifestyle publications (e.g. *ID*).

Recently there has been an increasing focus on means of public participation in computer-mediated communication. In Britain, Anne Campbell MP holds her constituency surgeries for Cambridge on-line. Further afield, American Vice-President Al Gore has promised that all Americans shall journey on the 'Information Superhighway', although at this point it is not quite clear whether the population will all be drivers or all passengers. The promise of such developments seems to indicate a desire to change the notions of citizenship and social participation. Authors such as Howard Rheingold have specifically highlighted the possibility of community formation, and in particular how social groups may be refashioned within 'virtual communities'. Rheingold has become known as an advocate for the kind of social networks and support which he describes as flourishing on systems such as The Well, a California-based group of users which he uses as one model of virtual community.7

As the arena which is covered by the term cyberspace expands, there is an increasing need to take account of the variety of spaces within the performance, and to specify which is the focus of attention for any given commentary. This paper is grounded in a corner of cyberspace which can best be described as Internet-based computer-mediated communication. Although this is not the only space in which cyberspace is performed, it does intersect with many of the cultural representations of cyberspace.8 One way of categorizing the activities within Internet-based computer-mediated communication is to use the socio-technical spaces which they inhabit: communication spaces (Listserv discussion lists, Usenet groups), interaction spaces (MU*s, Internet Relay Chat) and information spaces (World Wide Web, Gopher).9 Although the material which I use here is taken from a discussion list, which might be thought of purely as communication space, the performance of bodies on Sappho cross-cuts this three-part division of communication/interaction/information, reverberating through all the activities in this categorization and beyond.

It is at best optimistic to think that bodies can be tied to more stable definitions than cyberspace. As Julia Cream has shown the very idea of a body, and in particular a sexed body, is surrounded by ambiguity and contradiction.10 The encounter of bodies and cyberspace poses further contradictions for both performances. Bodies are intimately linked to our notions of who we are, our identities. Yet cyberspace is often portrayed as a place where *dis*embodiment is the norm. In Rheingold's words, 'People in virtual communities do just about everything people do in real life, but we leave our bodies behind'.11 It was this apparent paradox which led me to investigate where bodies were being created in cyberspace.

Much of recent cultural theory which has tackled the idea of the body and embodiment has been influenced by Judith Butler's formulation of performativity, and in particular the limitations of idealized conceptions of a binary opposition between the physical and the social body.12 Releasing ourselves from the restrictions of this idealization allows us to examine the boundary traffic between the social and physical performance. This is a concept of performance which, as stated above, I wish to apply strategically to both bodies and cyberspace in their textual appearances. Yet when the performance of bodies encounters cyberspace, the result often seems to be, in theory at least, a constructed dichotomy between the real and the virtual, reconfigured as the real permanent/physical/body versus the virtual/temporary/constructed body. The belief in this separation is reproduced in much of the commentary on cyberspace.

The bodily territory of cyberspace has been mapped for the most part by authors such as Rheingold who talks of a 'real physical body' on the one hand and separate 'virtual fluid identity' on the other.[13] Despite this statement, elsewhere in his own work Rheingold claims that his very being has been 'colonized' by cyberspace, and writes 'virtual communities inhabit my life' . This suggests that in practice it is hard to keep separate and oppositional the conceptions about 'real physical body' and the 'virtual fluid identity'.[14]

An alternative response to the difficulty of keeping discrete boundaries is to deny a place for the physical body in cyberspace at all. One way in which the physical body has been rejected is to claim that it has been surpassed by a newer more advanced model: the virtual body. In Arthur Kroker and Michael Weinstein's book *Data Trash* the new body is conceived as hypertexted.[15] The authors argue that the hypertexted body is at the forefront of social change and has anarchic and utopian interests. This body stands in dialectical opposition to a virtual class which itself is described as 'the post-historical successor to the early bourgeoisie of primitive capitalism'.[16] The hypertexted body is therefore at the centre of a virtual class war. For these authors the hypertexted body is a replacement for the so-called real flesh of out of date body types. Their dizzying predictions for the body are posed in the following terms:

> Refuse, then, nostalgia for the surpassed past of remaindered flesh, and hypertext your way to the (World Wide) Webbed body: the body that actually dances on its own data organs, sees with multimedia graphical interface screens, makes new best tele-friends on the MOO, writes electronic poetry on the disappearing edges of video, sound, and text integrators, and insists on going beyond the tedious world of binary divisions to the new cyber-mathematics of FITS. The hypertexted body, then, is the precursor of a new world of multimedia politics, fractalized economies, incept personalities, and (cybernetically) interfaced relationships.[17]

Although these premonitions are wide ranging and adventurous, Kroker and Weinstein never relinquish the security of the notion of opposing entities: the real 'remaindered flesh' body versus the virtual 'Webbed' body. Their conceptualization is limited by leaving this binary untouched, which is ironic given their comments on the 'tedious world of binary divisions'. Furthermore, in day-to-day e-mail interactions, on the Sappho discussion list at least, the body is not invoked as 'dancing on its own data organs' but rather it is employed strategically by referencing signals of lesbian identity, as will become clear below.

The sustained belief in the absence of the physical body, and the possibilities of disembodiment, have been celebrated by certain authors who claim potential possibilities for a liberating ambiguity of identity in cyberspace. Benedikt claims that: 'Egos and multiple egos, roles and functions, have a new existence in cyberspace.'[18] He believes that the absence of physical appearance, amongst other factors, leads to 'New, liquid and multiple associations between people. . .new modes and levels of truly interpersonal communication'.[19] Stone has hypothesized that this construction of disembodiment originates within and can be explained by the young male computer scientist culture which was the early playground in the origin myth of cyberspace. She suggests that the social and structural position of such young male computer scientists explains the wish for 'freedom from the sense of loss of control that accompanies adolescent male embodiment'.[20] However, this hypothesis is complicated by the discourse of female users and commentators, who think of the idea of detachment from the physical body as a virtue. For example, Alyssa Katz in the *Village Voice* suggested that by taking on an on-line male persona, women may 'experience the rush of beating men at the patriarchal game'. The apparent contradiction between Stone's reasoning about the desire for disembodiment as male, and Katz's readiness to abandon non-male gender, race, or physical appearance in order to surpass the male, might be partly explained by the different cultural meanings attached to embodiment, and in particular between bodies gendered as male and bodies gendered as female. Feminist theorists have convincingly argued that the body is not a playground for women (the metaphor often used of cyberspace), but a battleground.[21]

The media and publications industry flourishing around cyberspace as a commodity reflects similar fervour to abandon aspects of the body. The cry is: 'On-line, you can be anyone you want to be!'. In *The Observer* Jim McClellan wrote of cyberspace as a place in which total refashioning of the self is possible by rewriting bodily appearances. He used as his key example a cyberspace 'celebrity' who participated in on-line culture from a wheelchair at home, thus implying it was possible to surpass the body and 're-create yourself on-screen'.[22] The subject is quoted as saying: 'I literally transferred my social life into cyberspace, because I was forced to. I had complete mobility there.'[23] The text of the article was illustrated with a photograph portraying the interviewee in a wheelchair, holding a keyboard, suggesting a distorted mirroring of physical and virtual mobility.

Despite Kroker and Weinstein's abandonment of the 'surpassed past of the remaindered flesh', for the most part identity in cyberspace is presented in opposition to the abilities of the physical body. The way in which ideas about physical ability are integral to participation in virtual spaces is also highlighted in the anecdote of the male psychiatrist who presented himself as a woman with disabilities on a discussion list until exposed by other participants.[24] This tale is a fragment of the constantly reworked net myths and folklore. The crux of the story, the exposure, makes clear how assumptions about physical mobility and identity are shattered when 'true' gender is revealed. The pretence of being a woman also implies particular outcomes in terms of social and communicative mobility. The man's deceit was not just that he had sustained the idea of a woman's body, but that he had also used an image of disability in order to create a convincing on-line identity and develop relationships of trust with those who, as they testified, would not voluntarily have had the same kind of encounter with the body of a male psychiatrist. The comments of the female participants on the experience of the revelation of the 'real' body were expressed in terms of 'rape' and 'violation', implying some slippage between the categories of the physical and the virtual.

The experience of such deceit is a reminder that the body may be strategically performed rather than static and fixed. The evangelical claims of 'liberating fluidity' are complicated because of our expectations of responsibility and trust about the presentation of stable identity and an intelligible body. My focus is to examine the body in relation to gender and sexuality, since cyberspace itself is sexualized. In this performance gender, sex, and sexuality are collectively noticed or publicly forgotten. Previous research on Internet-based computer-mediated communication shows that the female body emerges as part of a problematic process in which women are forced to negotiate use as women, rather than as androgynous or as male.[25] This occurs across the spectrum of Internet-based computer-mediated communication, whether on Listserv discussion lists, Usenet groups, or in MU*s. Susan Herring found that after some time spent on e-mail lists her respondents would 'regularly infer the gender of message posters on the basis of features of these styles'.[26] Thus an idea of the 'real' gendered physical body behind the text was sustained. Gladys We has shown that women are more likely to problematize being a woman on-line than men are to problematize their own masculinity in the same spaces.[27] Furthermore Amy Bruckman's work on MUDs, which she characterizes as 'identity workshops', shows that being a woman is far more problematic than being a man because of the need to convince others that whatever your virtual body may be, your 'real' body is female.[28] Bruckman makes the point that male players are rarely if ever challenged about their maleness, but virtual women are standardly asked to try to *prove* that they have real physical female bodies.

This should not lead us to the assumption that there is an absence of images of women in cyberspace. The vast majority of Internet-based pornography and sex services are based around virtual access to parts of women's bodies. However, there is a marked difference in those sites where pictures of supposedly real women's silicone-aided bodies can be accessed and 'used', and computer-mediated communication in virtual textual environments. Whereas retrieving prescanned pictures of Page 3 models from sites in cyberspace does not require continual textual work by the user, participation in virtual environments, such as Internet Relay Chat sex channels, does require all participants to type their sexual fantasies continually in order to keep the channel operative. The image of female bodies is constantly reproduced on channels where women are eroticized. *.net* magazine readers were warned that in Internet Relay Chat sex channels: 'You'll probably be having netsex with a bloke, irrespective of whether the user name is Rebecca or Boris.'[29] The idea of a female body which has actually merged with the computer is also presented as potent and possible. The cover of the *.net* 'Virtual Love' issue portrays a wired woman. It shows the head of an apparently naked woman gazing at the reader. The background is pink and purple, scattered with flowers. On closer inspection it is evident that the woman's hair is mingled with wires, and it appears that they are firmly embedded in her scalp. The subtitle of this edition reads: 'Yes, it's the inevitable Sex and Romance issue.'

Such constructions of cyberspace confine and restrict women's bodies within a heterosexual framework. Men pretend to be women to attract the attention of 'real' women, who are in fact themselves other men pretending to be women. The practice of such cross-dressing does nothing to unsettle the assumption and practice of cyberspace as a process of heterosexuality. Thus the knowledge that in most contexts you will get much more attention by presenting yourself through text as a woman is used to subvert expectations, and to maintain a continual stream of virtual heterosexual interaction.

Not surprisingly, non-heterosexual performances are at the margins of cyberspace. Perhaps as a consequence many women who want to maintain identities which are not circumscribed by the norm of heterosexuality sometimes do so in clearly bounded environments such as closed discussion lists. Sappho is not the only list with lesbian content or a majority of lesbian-identified subscribers, although many of the other similar lists were created by subsets of subscribers from Sappho. There are local offshoots of Sappho on the East and West coasts of the USA and several European Sappho networks have recently been created. There are also unrelated lists on specific issues of interest to lesbians, such as parenting, or activist lists such as Queer Nation. As well as discussion lists there are several active Internet Relay Chat channels, and an increasing number of World Wide Web sites of lesbian interest, including pages for the Lesbian Avengers. One of the largest central information points for the resources for lesbians on the Internet is the Queer Resources Index, which because of its popularity has mirrors in several countries, to make access easier for those outside the USA. Nevertheless lesbian cyberspace is not always accessible to all users. For example in July 1995 America Online, probably the biggest commercial Internet provider in the USA, censored a set of World Wide Web pages with lesbian content.

Sappho produces a high volumes of messages per day, and many participants subscribe to a digested version of the list, which arrives as two to four e-mails per day, rather than between forty and one hundred individual messages, which is the alternative. It is difficult to estimate the average numbers of participants, but currently there two to three hundred subscribed e-mail addresses, ranging across educational, commercial, and non-profit organizations in North America, and to a lesser extent in Europe and Australia. Sappho is a closed discussion list, which means that an application to join must be sent to the 'list mistress' of either the regular or the digested version, and this message must include the specification that the would-be participant is female.

Sappho is similar to many other discussion lists in that it draws on and also sustains certain conventions of Internet-based textual exchanges such as formats for replying to messages from others, or the addition of emoticons to indicate non-verbal communication. Nancy Baym has shown in her work on rec.arts.tv.soaps how such groups create and sustain their own normative culture and history, including acronyms for frequently debated subjects.[30] In the same way, whereas certain common acronyms recur on Sappho (e.g. BTW for By The Way, or ROFL for Rolling On Floor Laughing), there are other Sappho-specific acronyms such as GBD, the Great Bisexual Debate, a reference to regular debates about the place of bisexuals within lesbian and gay movements and on the list itself.

Some of the textual activity on Sappho takes on a particular form because of the nature of the list. Sapphites also attempt to guess characteristics of the person from a post to the list, just as Herring described, even though on Sappho all the participants have sent a message saying that they identify as female. Kira Hall has shown that this process involves several specific factors: conforming to ideals of discursive femininity, an expectation of a female name, an anti-flaming policy, repeated discussion of overtly 'female' topics, a pro-separatist and pro-women attitude, and the use of feminist and/or lesbian signatures.[31] Postings which conform with these norms serve to confirm femaleness, a textual practice to indicate a physical body. In this way Sapphites, far from being disembodied, spend a considerable amount of time constructing an idea of a 'real' self and a 'physical' body.

Another difference from many other lists is the nature of the ideas which are constructed about community among Sapphites. Sappho is usually characterized as a safe space, a private arena in which views can be aired which might not necessarily be spoken elsewhere. Frequently the language of kinship is employed to describe this feeling of being ' home'. One Sapphite described the list as 'like family'. This is reflected in the range of the messages posted to Sappho, which includes general information, debates on current events, as well as updates on the state of health of partners, lovers, children, or pets. It is not uncommon for births, deaths, or other commemorative events to be announced to the whole list, and news updated frequently. This contributes to a list character which is very different to a list which is focused on one particular topic, such the one described in Baym's study of soap opera fans. Sappho permits another place called 'home' for those identifying as lesbian or bisexual, for whom the notion of the 'real' domestic setting may be fragmentary and contradictory.[32]

Hall emphasized the feminist or lesbian signature as one part of the screening process which persuaded others of a convincing performance of a lesbian body in cyberspace. It is not obligatory to include a signature at the end of an e-mail message, but many participants do use several lines at the end of their post to provide more personal details, such as name, address, or a favourite quotation. Many of the signatures at the end of Sapphites' messages include the words of prominent figures in lesbian culture, largely drawn from the context of North America. For example a signature might include the words of Adrienne Rich, Audre Lorde, k d lang, or Melissa Etheridge.

The lesbian body may also be coded in the signature, providing another means of screening a 'real' body. The Muff Diva Index (MDI), often included in the last line of the signature, encapsulates the textual bodywork of participants. Thus an image of a lesbian body on Sappho might appear as follows:

MDI: FB! H * M * TE B! O!

At first glance this looks like a jumble of letters and other ASCII characters, but in fact each segment relates to a certain construction of the lesbian body. Each letter signifies a particular aspect of the code. The first factor is the Femme-Butch factor (FB), followed by a code of the measure of where along the dimension of Femme-Butch the participant codes herself. The scale of the dimension runs from !!! to *** as follows: !!!, !!, !, blank, *, **, *** (although the extremes of the scale are not used with certain factors). The other factors in the segment of code which I have reproduced above represent hair length (H), muscle tone (M), trendy-earthy (TE), boots-heels versus sandals-sneakers (B), Olivia music (O).[33] From the decoding list which specifies the precise characteristics of each point of the scale, this piece of MDI could be read as a Sapphite who describes herself as (FB) 'butchish, but with a femmy side'; (H) 'hair short with a couple of sexy waves'; (M)'muscles softish, roundish'; (TE)'Trendy and Earthy in equal amounts'; (B) 'wears boots/heels most of the time, rather than sandals/sneakers'; (O) 'doesn't care for Olivia records-type music, but will listen if girlfriend puts it on the stereo'.

This list of factors is not exhaustive, and it would be deceptive to present such textual bodywork as static, since the code and ways of decoding are continually changing. Refashioning the MDI is a communal process within which new factors are being added and existing ones refined, both publicly on Sappho, and privately between individual participants. The MDI is occasionally posted to the whole list, but the usual way to obtain the decoding frame is to post a request publicly to the whole list or privately to a participant who included an MDI in her signature.

The MDI encapsulates outward signs of a lesbian body. It combines the physical and the social via technology; thus hair length and muscle tone which are usually recognized as physical characteristics are set alongside cultural indicators such as the Olivia music factor. Other factors are harder to classify, and the ambiguity of the FB factor becomes apparent—does this relate to a dress code, or an attitude, or a culturally specific performance, or a mixture of any of these? Although the MDI is a textual performance, some of those who have scanned images of themselves to put on Web pages retain a MDI index in their signature, adding the address for their Web page underneath. The fact that the MDI is not replaced by a scanned photograph but works in conjunction with it indicates its importance as a coded label within a boundary story of bodies, sexuality, and cyberspace, rather than just a textual representation where graphical images were not possible. Through the use of the MDI, bodies on Sappho actively subvert the norm of dominant heterosexuality in computer-mediated communication by the use of references to lesbian cultural practices, while retaining an aura of exclusion by encrypting these practices. Yet once the MDI is decoded, and the participant has been through the screening process discussed by Hall, she may join the process of suggesting new segments of code or refining existing ones.

I began this paper by showing why I had first problematized the appearance of my own body on Internet-based computer-mediated communication. I have suggested that it might be beneficial to think of both bodies and cyberspace as strategically performed. The performance of the body in the MDI shows the fragile boundaries of the body in itself (where does it end? what is the physical? what is the social?) as well as how it is reproduced in cyberspace. From the practices of the MDI we could think about the process of *doing* cyberspace as in itself embodied, even though cyberspace is often presented as the space of disembodied identity. Notions of embodiment and embodied experience have been extensively discussed within feminist theory and cultural studies, but they might also provide fruitful lines of enquiry within the study of computer-mediated communication, particularly where this enquiry seeks to be grounded in the daily practices of those who participate in Internet-based communication. This might lead us to abandon the opposition of the 'real' and the 'virtual', and at the very least be vigilant about the social and political implications of a rhetoric of disembodiment and liberation, given that some performers of cyberspace are working so hard to sustaining their marginal textual bodies.

Notes

1. Although Sappho is a discussion list which advertises itself as open to all women, it is assumed by participants that the majority on the list are lesbian or bisexual women, and this is reflected in the content of the posts.
2. See Donna J. Haraway, *Simians, Cyborgs and Women: The Reinvention of Women* (London: Routledge and Kegan Paul, 1991); and Allucquere Rosanne Stone, 'Will the Real Body Please Stand Up? Boundary Stories about Virtual Cultures', in *Cyberspace: First Steps*, ed. Michael Benedikt (Cambridge: MIT Press, 1992).
3. Donna J. Haraway, 'A Cyborg Manifesto: Science, Technology and Socialist-Feminism in the Late Twentieth Century', in Haraway (1991), 181.
4. See Howard Rheingold, *The Virtual Community: Homesteading on the Electronic Frontier* (Reading: Addison-Wesley, 1993); Douglas Rushkoff, *Cyberia: Life in the Trenches of Hyperspace* (London: Flamingo, 1994); J. C. Herz, *Surfing on the Internet : A Net-Head's Adventures On-Line* (London: Abacus, 1994).
5. See Benedikt (1992).
6. Ibid. 1-3.
7. See Rheingold (1993).
8. See those given in Rheingold (1993), Rushkoff (1994), and Herz (1994) as well as the scope of articles in Steven G. Jones, ed., *Cybersociety: Computer Mediated Communication and Community* (London: Sage, 1995).
9. For further explanation of these spaces see John December, 'Transitions in Studying Computer-Mediated Communication' in *Computer-Mediated Communication Magazine* 2.1 (1995).
10. See Julia Cream, 'Re-solving Riddles: The Sexed Body' in Bell, David, and Gill Valentine, eds., *Mapping Desire* (London: Routledge and Kegan Paul, 1995), 31-40.
11. Rheingold (1993), 3.
12. Judith Butler, *Gender Trouble* (New York: Routledge and Kegan Paul, 1989), and *Bodies That Matter: On the discursive limits of 'sex'* (New York: Routledge and Kegan Paul, 1993).
13. See Rheingold (1993).
14. Ibid. 10.
15. Arthur Kroker and Michael Weinstein, *Data Trash: The Theory of the Virtual Class* (New York: St Martin's Press, 1994).
16. Ibid. 18.
17. Ibid. 18.
18. See Benedikt (1992), 123.
19. Ibid. 123.
20. See Stone (1992).

21. See Susan Bordo, 'Material Girl: The Effacements of Postmodern Culture', in L. Goldstein, ed., *The Female Body: Figures, Styles, Speculations* (Ann Arbor: University of Michigan Press, 1991).
22. *The Observer* (Life Section), 13 February 1994, 8.
23. Ibid. 8.
24. See Stone (1992) 82-3; the original report appeared in MS.
25. This explains in part the strategy by some participants of attempting to disguise gender by choosing a username which is thought to be 'gender free'.
26. Susan C. Herring, 'Gender and Democracy in Computer-Mediated Communication', in *Electronic Journal of Communication*, 3.2 (1993).
27. Gladys We, 'Cross Gender Communication in Cyberspace' in *The Arachnet Electronic Journal on Virtual Culture*, 2.3 (1994).
28. Amy S. Bruckman, 'Gender Swapping on the Internet', unpublished manuscript, 1992. Available via anonymous ftp from media.mit.edu in pub/MediaMOO/Papers/identity -workshop.
29. *.net* magazine, February 1994, 42.
30. Nancy K. Baym, 'The Emergence of Community in Computer-Mediated Communication', in Jones (1995).
31. Kira Hall, 'Cyberfeminism', in Susan Herring, ed., *Computer-mediated Communication* (Amsterdam, John Benjamins, in press).
32. Lynda Johnston and Gill Valentine, 'Wherever I Lay my Girlfriend, That's My Home: The Performance and Surveillance of Lesbian Identities in Domestic Environments', in Bell and Valentine (1995), 99-113.
33. Olivia was the first lesbian-owned national record label to release music by lesbians for lesbians in the 1970s-1980s, including artists Meg Christian, Holly Near, and Chris Williamson.

Notes on Contributors

Michael Allen is multimedia developer for the TLTP-funded 'CAL in the Humanities' project at the University of East Anglia, and has recently taken up a position as Research Officer at the British Film Institute. His doctoral thesis was on the later feature films of D. W. Griffith, and forthcoming publications include the 'Technology' section of the revised *The Cinema Book*. His research interests include early cinema, the history of media technologies, and multimedia.

Laura Chernaik is Lecturer in American Studies at the University of Nottingham. Her research interests are in feminist theories of gender, sexuality, race, and class; the relation between transnationalism, postmodernity, and postmodernism; and Science Fiction Studies. She has published articles in *Renaissance and Modern Studies*, *Letterature d'America*, and *Gender, Place and Culture*.

Warren Chernaik is Programme Director of the Centre for English Studies and Reader in English Literature at Queen Mary and Westfield College, University of London. He is author of *Sexual Freedom in Restoration Literature* (Cambridge UP, 1995), *The Poet's Time: Religion and Politics in the Work of Andrew Marvell* (Cambridge University Press, 1983), and *The Poetry of Limitation: A Study of Edmund Waller* (Yale University Press, 1968), and co-editor of *Modernist Writers and the Marketplace* (London: Macmilllan, 1996) and a previous volume in this series, *The Politics of the Electronic Text* (1993). Since the publication of this last collection of essays, he has advanced technologically from a manual typewriter to an antique PC.

Marilyn Deegan was Director of the CTI Centre for Textual Studies and Office for Humanities Communication until September 1995, when she took up the post of Professor of Electronic Library Research in the Humanities at De Montfort University, where she is also Co-Director of the Institute for Electronic Library Research. Professor Deegan has published widely on humanities computing topics, and she is also known for her work on Anglo-Saxon medical manuscripts. Her latest project, which will be published at the end of 1996, is an edition of John Buchan's novel *The Dancing Floor* for OUP's World's Classics series.

Andrew Gibson is Senior Lecturer in English Literature at Royal Holloway, University of London, where he runs the MA in Post-modernism, Literature and Contemporary Culture. He is also founder and organizer of the London University Seminar for Research into Joyce's *Ulysses*. He is author of *Reading Narrative Discourse: Studies in the Novel from Cervantes to Beckett* (London: Macmillan, 1995) and *Towards a*

Postmodern Theory of Narrative, to be published by Edinburgh University Press in their Postmodern Theory series later in 1996. He is also editor of *Reading Joyce's 'Circe'* (European Joyce Studies series, Atlanta and Amsterdam, 1994) and *Joyce's 'Ithaca'* (forthcoming in the European Studies series in 1996). He is currently writing a book on Postmodern ethics and the novel.

George Landow is Professor of English and Art History at Brown University. He has written and lectured internationally on nineteenth century literature, art, religion as well as on literary theory, educational computing, and digital culture. His published works include *Hypertext: The Convergence of Contemporary Critical Theory and Technology* (Johns Hopkins University Press, 1992); *The Digital Word: Text-Based Computing in the Humanities* (with Paul Delaney, MIT, 1993), and *Hypertext in Hypertext* (Johns Hopkins University Press, 1994), an expanded electronic version of *Hypertext*. Since 1985 he has worked as a member of the team at the Institute for Research in Information and Scholarship that developed Intermedia at Brown University. Examples of his work may be invoked at http://www.stg.brown.edu/projects/hypertext/landow/cv/landow_ov.html

John Pickering is Lecturer in Psychology at Warwick University. Although his research background is in cognitive science he maintains a strong interest in the biological and cultural production of consciousness. His present research is directed towards the interaction of psychology with recent continental philosophy and critical theory. He is particularly interested in how technology is incorporated into the human psychological condition.

Sadie Plant is a Faculty Research Fellow associated with the Cybernetic Culture Research Unit of the Department of Philosophy at Warwick University. Her current research interests include antihumanist philosophy and cybernetic culture; the work of Foucault, Debord, Deleuze and Guattari, and Irigaray; contemporary developments in non-linear dynamics, film, music, multimedia, and telecommunications; and the future of feminism and sexuality. Recent publications include *The Most Radical Gesture: The Situationist International in a Postmodern Age* (London: Routledge and Kegan Paul, 1992) and *Zeros and Ones* (London: Fourth Estate and Doubleday, 1996).

Kathryn Sutherland is Professor of Modern English Literature at the University of Nottingham. She has published widely on literature of the romantic period, on literature and economics, and on electronic textuality. She is academic director of the Electra Project.

Nina Wakeford is Lecturer in Sociology at Sheffield University. She currently holds an ESRC Postdoctoral Fellowship to study women's experiences of computer-mediated communication. Her research interests, on which she has published a number of articles, include gender and technology, and diversity in Cyberspace.

Office for Humanities Communication Publications

This volume is the seventh in a series of publications concerned with the impact of computers in humanities scholarship and higher education. The OHC is funded by the British Library Research and Development Department. Publications in this series are aimed at scholars who, while expert in their own field, may know little about computers, and the following is a list of current titles in the series.

Computers and Language
Edited by Caroline Davis and Marilyn Deegan

A collection of ten papers originally given at the conference 'Computers and Language II' at Sheffield City Polytechnic in September 1991. A unifying theme in the collection is how to go about teaching language and literature by computer. Practical experiences of integrating computers in Modern Language and English Literature courses are described. Computer-based language learning in a business and commercial context is discussed, and there are also papers on the use of the computer in teaching ancient and medieval languages.

December 1992   £10.00

The Politics of the Electronic Text
Edited by Warren Chernaik, Caroline Davis and Marilyn Deegan

The proceedings of a one day conference, 'The Politics of the Electronic Text', held on 12th February 1993 at the Centre for English Studies at the University of London. The conference addressed the opportunites and difficulties created by the impact of new technology on scholarship. Electronic texts, corpora, and hypertext are bringing about changes in scholarly practices and in attitudes to texts and criticism, as well as raising problems in the rights of control over texts, pricing structures, and copyright law.

July 1993   £5.00

The Digitization of Primary Textual Sources
Peter Robinson

This report reviews work done by individual scholars and projects in digitizing manuscript images and the technologies currently available. It makes positive recommendations as to how digitizing might proceed in the short term, with suggestions as to what methods of digitization might be appropriate to particular materials. It also indicates problems to be solved in the long term. Four colour plates give examples of digitization processes.

August 1993   Reprinted December 1994   £10.00

The *Canterbury Tales* Project: Occasional Papers I
Edited by Norman Blake and Peter Robinson

The *Canterbury Tales* Project aims to recover the transmission history of the *Tales* by transcription, collation, and analysis of all the extant manuscripts. The Occasional Papers volumes collect essays relating to this aim. This volume contains papers on editing the *Tales*, transcription for the computer, computer-assisted stemmatic analysis, a new manuscript catalogue, and the glosses in the textual tradition.

December 1993   £10.00

The Transcription of Primary Textual Sources Using SGML
Peter Robinson

This report explains the recommendations of the Text Encoding Initiative for transcription of primary sources, based on Standard Generalized Markup Language. There is liberal use of worked examples of coding of real texts. The report is intended to enable scholars beginning new projects, or working on existing projects to use the TEI proposals in the preparation of electronic versions of primary texts.

April 1994   £5.00

Copies can be obtained from The Office for Humanities Communication, Humanities Computing Unit, Oxford University Computing Services, 13 Banbury Road, Oxford OX2 6NN, enclosing cheque made payable to Oxford University Computing Services. Addition for postage and packing per copy: £1.00 UK, £2.00 Europe, and £3.00 outside Europe.

DATE DUE

OhioLINK			
APR 21 REC'D			
MAY 0 6 1999			
APR 22 REC'D			
OhioLINK			
MAR 2 1 REC'D			
LINK			
NOV 1 3 REC'D			
AUG 1 6 2004			
MAY 1 6 2005			
MAY 1 6 REC'D			
GAYLORD			PRINTED IN U.S.A.

Z 1033 .E43 B49 1996

Beyond the book